**ARRL's**

D1636284

# GEN
# Q&A

## Upgrade to a **General Class**
## **Ham Radio License!**

### Sixth Edition

**By Ward Silver, NØAX**

**Contributing Editor:**
Mark Wilson, K1RO

**Editorial Assistant:**
Maty Weinberg, KB1EIB

**Production Staff:**

David Pingree, N1NAS, Senior Technical Illustrator

Jodi Morin, KA1JPA, Assistant Production Supervisor: Layout

Sue Fagan, KB1OKW, Graphic Design Supervisor: Cover Design

Michelle Bloom, WB1ENT, Production Supervisor

**Cover photo:**

Nolan Palmer, KC1IEO, is seen on the air from a special event
station at the 2018 ARRL New England Division Convention held
in Boxborough, Massachusetts. Nolan is a member of the Sci-Tech
Amateur Radio Society (**www.STARS.radio**), a radio club made
up of students, their families, and other supportive radio amateurs
from throughout New England.

**ARRL** The national association for
**AMATEUR RADIO**®
225 Main Street, Newington, CT 06111-1400
**www.arrl.org**

This book may be used for General license exams given beginning July 1, 2019. *QST* and the ARRL website (**www.arrl.org**) will have news about any rules changes affecting the General class license or any of the material in this book.

**Feedback:** We're interested in hearing your comments on this book and what you'd like to see in future editions. Please email comments to us at **pubsfdbk@arrl.org**, including your name, call sign, email address, and the title, edition, and printing of this book.

We strive to produce books without errors. Sometimes mistakes do occur, however. When we become aware of problems in our books (other than obvious typographical errors), we post corrections on the ARRL website. If you think you have found an error, please check **www.arrl.org** for corrections and supplemental material. If you don't find a correction there, please let us know by sending email to **pubsfdbk@arrl.org**.

# Contents

# Foreword

**Congratulations and welcome**! If you have decided to upgrade to the General class Amateur Radio license or are thinking about giving it a try, this book will help. Upgrading to General will open up the world of shortwave communications and a wide range of Amateur Radio bands and modes and activities — you won't regret it! For more than 100 years, the ARRL has helped Amateur Radio operators get the most out of their hobby by advancing their operating and technical skills. You'll find the ARRL license preparation materials to be the most complete package available. They will help you do much more than just pass the written exam.

All of the information you need to pass the Element 3 General class written exam is here in the sixth edition of *ARRL's General Q&A*. Each and every question in the General class examination question pool is addressed with study material that explains the correct answer and provides background information. If you can answer the questions in this book, you can pass the written exam with confidence.

A companion to this book, *The ARRL General Class License Manual*, helps you understand the electronics theory, operating practices and FCC rules. This not only helps you pass the exam, but makes you more confident on the air and serves as a reference after you have upgraded. The online *ARRL Exam Review for Ham Radio* allows you to take randomly generated practice exams using questions from the actual examination question pool. Go to **www.arrl.org/examreview**.

If you'd like to take part in one of Amateur Radio's great traditions (and have a lot of fun, too), the ARRL offers training resources, on-the-air code practice and even a code-practice oscillator kit training for learning the Morse code. While Morse proficiency is no longer required for you to get an Amateur Radio license, it remains quite popular with amateurs for its efficiency and simple elegance.

Visit the ARRL's comprehensive website at **www.arrl.org** and browse the latest news about Amateur Radio, tap into the wealth of services provided by the

ARRL and look through the ARRL online catalog for publications and supplies to support any activity.

The sixth edition of *ARRL's General Q&A* is the product of cooperation between readers of the ARRL study materials and the ARRL staff. You can help make this book better by providing your own feedback. After you have passed your exam, please send your suggestions, questions and comments by email to **pubsfdbk@arrl.org**. Comments from readers are very important in making subsequent editions more effective and useful to readers.

Thanks for making the decision to upgrade — we hope to hear you on the air soon, using your new General class privileges and enjoying more of Amateur Radio. Good luck!

Ward Silver, NØAX
St. Charles, Missouri
March 2019

New Ham Desk
ARRL Headquarters
225 Main Street
Newington, CT
06111-1494
860-594-0200

Prospective new amateurs call:
**800-32-NEW-HAM (800-326-3942)**

You can also contact us via e-mail:
**newham@arrl.org**

or check out
**www.arrl.org**

# What is
# Amateur Radio?

Perhaps you've just picked up this book in the library or at a bookstore and are wondering what this Amateur Radio business is all about. Maybe you have a friend or relative who is a "ham" and you're interested in becoming one, as well. In any case, a short explanation is in order.

Amateur Radio or "ham radio" is one of the longest-lived wireless activities. Amateur experimenters were operating right along with Marconi in the early part of the 20th century. They helped advance the state-of-the-art in radio, television, wireless data and dozens of other communications services right up to the present day. There are more than 700,000 "hams" in the United States alone and several million more around the world!

Amateur Radio in the United States is a federally regulated *communications service*, administered by the Federal Communications Commission or FCC. Created officially in 1934, the amateur service is intended to promote electronics and radio experimentation, provide emergency backup communications, encourage private citizens to train and practice operating, and even spread goodwill through person-to-person contacts over the airwaves.

**Field Day is the largest event in Amateur Radio as thousands of North American hams operate from portable stations to train for public service communications. Field Day is a great opportunity to try different activities and introduce others to ham radio.**

## Who Is a Ham and What Do Hams Do?

Anyone can be a ham — there are no age limits or physical requirements that prevent anyone from passing their license exam and getting on the air. Kids as young as 5 years old have passed the basic exam and there are hams over the age of 100. You probably fall somewhere in that range!

Once you get on the air and start meeting other hams, you'll find many capabilities and interests. Of course, there are many technically skilled hams who work as engineers, scientists or technicians. But just as many don't have a deep technical background. You're just as likely to encounter writers, public safety personnel, students, farmers, truck drivers — anyone with an interest in personal communications over the radio.

The activities of Amateur Radio are incredibly varied. Amateurs who hold the Technician class license — the usual first license for hams in the US — communicate primarily with local and regional amateurs using relay stations called *repeaters*. Known as "Techs," they sharpen their operating skills, use mobile and portable equipment, and often join public service teams. They may focus on the burgeoning wireless data networks assembled and used by hams around the world. Techs can make use of the growing number of Amateur Radio satellites, built and launched by hams along with the commercial "birds." Technicians transmit their own television signals, push the limits of signal propagation through the atmosphere and experiment with microwaves. Hams hold most of the world records for long-distance communication on microwave frequencies, in fact!

**Responding after Hurricane Maria in 2017, Amateur Radio operators traveled to Puerto Rico to provide communications in support of the Red Cross and other disaster relief activites.**

Hams who advance or *upgrade* to General class are granted additional privileges to use the frequencies usually associated with shortwave operation. This is the traditional Amateur Radio you may have encountered in movies or books. On these frequencies, signals travel worldwide, so General and Extra class amateurs can make direct contact with foreign hams. No internet, phone systems, or data networks are required. It's just you, your radio, and the ionosphere — the upper layers of the Earth's atmosphere!

Many hams use voice, Morse code, and computer-based digital modes to communicate, engaging in conversation, participating in competitions, and exchanging text and images. All of these signals are mixed together on the frequencies where hams operate, making the experience of tuning a radio receiver through the crowded bands an interesting experience.

One thing common to all hams is that all of their operation is noncommercial, especially the volunteers who provide emergency communications. Hams pursue their hobby purely for personal enjoyment and to advance their skills, taking satisfaction from providing services to their fellow citizens. This is especially valuable after natural disasters such as hurricanes and earthquakes when commercial systems are knocked out for a while. Amateur operators are activated to provide backup communication for hours, days, weeks or even months until the regular systems are restored. All this from a little study and a simple exam!

## Want to Find Out More?

If you'd like to find out more about Amateur Radio in general, there is lots of information available on the Internet. A good place to start is on the American Radio Relay League's (ARRL) ham radio introduction page, **www.arrl.org/what-is-ham-radio**. Books such as *Ham Radio for Dummies* and others at **www.arrl.org/shop/Beginners** will help you "fill in the blanks" as you learn more.

Supported by books and web pages, there is no better way to learn about ham radio than to meet your local amateur operators. It is quite likely that no matter where you live in the United States, there is a ham radio club in your area — perhaps several! The ARRL provides a club lookup web page at **www.arrl.org/find-a-club** where you can find a club just by entering your ZIP code or state. Carrying on the tradition of mutual assistance, many clubs make helping newcomers understand and enjoy ham radio a part of their charter.

Hams are confident that you'll find their activities interesting. Amateur Radio is much more than just talking on a radio as you'll find out. It's an opportunity to dive into the fascinating world of radio communications, electronics and computers as deeply as you wish to go. Welcome!

# When to Expect New Books

A Question Pool Committee (QPC) consisting of representatives from the various Volunteer Examiner Coordinators (VECs) prepares the license question pools. The QPC establishes a schedule for revising and implementing new Question Pools. The current Question Pool revision schedule is as follows:

| Question Pool | Current Study Guides | Valid Through |
|---|---|---|
| **Technician** (Element 2) | *The ARRL Ham Radio License Manual*, 4th Edition  *ARRL's Tech Q&A*, 7th Edition | June 30, 2022 |
| **General** (Element 3) | *The ARRL General Class License Manual*, 9th edition  *ARRL's General Q&A*, 6th Edition | June 30, 2023 |
| **Amateur Extra** (Element 4) | *The ARRL Extra Class License Manual*, 11th Edition  *ARRL's Extra Q&A*, 4th Edition | June 30, 2020 |

As new question pools are released, ARRL will produce new study materials before the effective date of the new pools. Until then, the current question pools will remain in use and current ARRL study materials, including this book, will help you prepare for your exam.

As the new question pool schedules are confirmed, the information will be published in *QST* and on the ARRL website at **www.arrl.org**.

# How to Use
## This Book

To earn a General class Amateur Radio license, you must pass (or receive credit for) FCC Elements 2 (Technician class) and 3 (General class). This book is designed to help you prepare for and pass the Element 3 written exam. If you do not already have a Technician class license, you will need study materials for the Element 2 (Technician) exam.

The Element 3 exam consists of 35 questions about Amateur Radio rules, theory and practice, as well as some basic electronics. A passing grade is 74%, so you must answer 26 of the 35 questions correctly.

*ARRL's General Q&A* has 10 sections that follow subelements G1 through G0 in the General class syllabus. The questions and multiple choice answers in this book are printed exactly as they will appear on your exam. (Be careful, though. The position of the answers may be scrambled from that of the actual exam so you won't be able to simply memorize an answer letter for each question.) In this book, the letter of the correct answer is printed in **boldface** type just before the explanation.

The ARRL also maintains a special web page for General class students at **www.arrl.org/general-class-license-manual**. The useful and interesting on-line references and other supplemental information listed there put you one click away from related and useful information. Be sure to visit that web page during your preparation for the exam.

If you are taking a licensing class, help your instructors by letting them know about areas in which you need help. They want you to learn as thoroughly and quickly as possible, so don't hold back with your questions. Similarly, if you find the material particularly clear or helpful, tell them that, too, so it can be used in the next class!

### What We Assume About You

You don't have to be a technical guru or an expert operator to upgrade to General class! As you progress through the material, you'll build on the basic science of radio and electricity you mastered for Technician. No advanced mathematics is required and tutorials are listed at **www.arrl.org/general-class-license-manual**. As with the Technician license, mastering rules and regulations will require learning some new words and a few numbers. You should have a basic calculator, which you'll also be allowed to use during the license exam.

If you have some background in radio, perhaps as a technician or trained operator, you may be able to skip over some of the sections. It's common for technically-minded students to focus on the rules and regulations while students with an operating background tend to need the technical material more. Whichever you may be, be sure that you can answer the questions because any of them may be on the test!

*ARRL's General Q&A* can be used either by an individual student, studying on his or her own, or as part of a licensing class taught by an instructor. If you're part of a class, the instructor will set the order in which the material is covered. The solo student can move at any pace and in any convenient order. You'll find that having a friend to study with makes learning the material more fun as you help each other over the rough spots.

Don't hesitate to ask for help! If you can't find the answer in the book or at the website, email your question to the ARRL's New Ham Desk, **newham@arrl.org**. The ARRL's experts will answer directly or connect you with another ham that can answer your questions.

## Online Practice Exams

While you're studying and when you feel like you're ready for the actual exam you can get some good practice by taking an on-line Amateur Radio exams. The exams are free and you can take them over and over again in complete privacy. To get started, visit the *ARRL Exam Review for Ham Radio* web page at **www.arrl.org/examreview**.

These exams are quite realistic and you get quick feedback about the questions you didn't answer correctly. When you find yourself passing the practice exams by a comfortable margin, you'll be ready for the real thing!

# Testing
## Process

When you're ready, you'll need to find a test session. If you're in a licensing class, the instructor will help you find and register for a session. Otherwise, you can find a test session by using the ARRL's web page for finding exams, **www. arrl.org/exam**. If you can register for the test session in advance, do so. Other sessions, such as those at hamfests or conventions, are available to anyone that shows up or walk-ins. You may have to wait for an available space though, so go early!

As for all amateur exams, the General class exam is administered by Volunteer Examiners (VEs). All VEs are certified by a Volunteer Examiner Coordinator (VEC) such as the ARRL VEC. A VEC trains and certifies VEs and processes the FCC paperwork for their test sessions.

Bring your original current license or Certificate of Successful Completion of Examination (CSCE) and a photocopy (to send with the application). You'll need two forms of identification including at least one photo ID, such as a driver's license, passport or employer's identity card. Know your Social Security Number (SSN). You can bring pencils or pens, blank scratch paper and a calculator, but any kind of computer or on-line device is prohibited.

The FCC allows Volunteer Examiners to use a range of procedures to accommodate applicants with various disabilities. If this applies to you, you'll still have to pass the test, but special exam procedures are available. Contact your local VE team or the Volunteer Examiner Coordinator (VEC) responsible for the test session you'll be attending. Or contact the ARRL/VEC Office at 225 Main St, Newington CT 06111-1494 or by phone at 860-594-0200.

Once you're signed in, you'll need to fill out a copy of the National Conference of Volunteer Examiner Coordinator's (NCVEC) Quick Form 605. This is an application for a new or upgraded license. It is used only at test sessions and for a VEC to process a license renewal or a license change. Do not use an NCVEC Quick Form 605 for any kind of application directly to the FCC — it will be rejected. After filling out the form, pay the current test fee and get ready. Good luck!

### The Exam

The General test takes from 30 minutes to an hour. You will be given a question booklet and an answer sheet. Be sure to read the instructions, fill in all the necessary information and sign your name wherever it's required. Check to be sure your booklet has all the questions and be sure to mark the answer in the correct space for each question.

You don't have to answer the questions in order — skip the hard ones and go back to them. If you read the answers carefully, you'll probably find that you can eliminate one or more "distracters." Of the remaining answers, only one will be the best. If you can't decide which is the correct answer, go ahead and guess. There is no penalty for an incorrect guess. When you're done, go back and check your answers and double-check your arithmetic — there's no rush!

Once you've answered all 35 questions, the Volunteer Examiners will grade and verify your test results. Assuming you've passed (congratulations!) you'll fill

# NCVEC QUICK-FORM 605 APPLICATION
## AMATEUR OPERATOR/PRIMARY STATION LICENSE

### SECTION 1 - TO BE COMPLETED BY APPLICANT | PLEASE PRINT LEGIBLY!

**PRINT LAST NAME:** Grimaldi
**SUFFIX (Jr., Sr.):**
**FIRST NAME:** Amanda
**M.I.:**
**STATION CALL SIGN (IF ANY):** N1NHL

**MAILING ADDRESS (Number and Street or P.O. Box):** 225 main St

**CITY:** Newington
**STATE CODE:** CT
**ZIP CODE (5 or 9 Numbers):** 06111
**FEDERAL REGISTRATION NUMBER (FRN) - IF NONE, THEN SOCIAL SECURITY NUMBER (SSN):** 0005189337

**DAYTIME TELEPHONE NUMBER (Include Area Code):** 860-594-0200
**E-MAIL ADDRESS (MANDATORY TO RECEIVE LICENSE NOTIFICATION EMAIL FROM FCC):** agrimaldi@arrl.net

**Basic Qualification Question:** *ANSWER REQUIRED IN ORDER TO PROCESS YOUR APPLICATION*

Has the Applicant or any party to this application, or any party directly or indirectly controlling the Applicant, ever been convicted of a felony by any state or federal court? ☐ YES ☒ NO

If "YES," see "FCC BASIC QUALIFICATION QUESTION INSTRUCTIONS AND PROCEDURES" on the back of this form.

**I HEREBY APPLY FOR** (Make an X in the appropriate box(es)):

☐ **EXAMINATION** for a new license grant

☒ **EXAMINATION** for **upgrade** of my license class

☐ **CHANGE** my **name** on my license to my new name
Former Name: _____
(Last name) (Suffix) (First name) (MI)

☐ **CHANGE** my mailing address to **above** address

☐ **CHANGE** my station **call sign** systematically
Applicant's Initials: To confirm _____

☐ **RENEWAL** of my license grant
Exp. Date: _____

**Do you have another license application on file with the FCC which has not been acted upon?**
**PURPOSE OF OTHER APPLICATION**
**PENDING FILE NUMBER (FOR VEC USE ONLY)**

**I certify that:**
- I waive any claim to the use of any particular frequency regardless of prior use by license or otherwise;
- All statements and attachments are true, complete and correct to the best of my knowledge and belief and are made in good faith;
- I am not a representative of a foreign government;
- I am not subject to a denial of Federal benefits pursuant to Section 5301 of the Anti-Drug Abuse Act of 1988, 21 U.S.C. § 862;
- The construction of my station will NOT be an action which is likely to have a significant environmental effect (See 47 CFR Sections 1.1301-1.1319 and Section 97.13(a));
- I have read and WILL COMPLY with Section 97.13(c) of the Commission's Rules regarding RADIOFREQUENCY (RF) RADIATION SAFETY and the amateur service section of OST/OET Bulletin Number 65.

**Signature of Applicant:**
X _Amanda Grimaldi_
**Date Signed:** 1/23/2019

### SECTION 2 - TO BE COMPLETED BY ALL ADMINISTERING VEs

**Applicant is qualified for operator license class:**

☐ **NO NEW LICENSE OR UPGRADE WAS EARNED**

☐ **TECHNICIAN** — Element 2

☒ **GENERAL** — Elements 2 and 3

☐ **AMATEUR EXTRA** — Elements 2, 3 and 4

**DATE OF EXAMINATION SESSION:** 01-23-2019
**EXAMINATION SESSION LOCATION:** Newington CT
**VEC ORGANIZATION:** ARRL
**VEC RECEIPT DATE:**

I CERTIFY THAT I HAVE COMPLIED WITH THE ADMINISTERING VE REQUIRMENTS IN PART 97 OF THE COMMISSION'S RULES AND WITH THE INSTRUCTIONS PROVIDED BY THE COORDINATING VEC AND THE FCC.

| | VEs NAME (Print First, MI, Last, Suffix) | VEs STATION CALL SIGN | VEs SIGNATURE (Must match name) | DATE SIGNED |
|---|---|---|---|---|
| 1st | Maria Somma | AB1FM | Maria Somma | 01-23-2019 |
| 2nd | PERRY T GREEN | WY1O | Perry Green | 01-23-2019 |
| 3rd | Penny Harts | N1NAG | Penny Harts | 01-23-2019 |

DO NOT SEND THIS FORM TO FCC – THIS IS NOT AN FCC FORM.
IF THIS FORM IS SENT TO FCC, FCC WILL RETURN IT TO YOU WITHOUT ACTION.

NCVEC FORM 605 - March 2018
FOR VE/VEC USE ONLY - Page 1

This sample NCVEC Quick Form 605 shows how your form will look after you have completed your upgrade to General.

out a Certificate of Successful Completion of Examination. The exam organizers will submit your results to the FCC while you keep the CSCE as evidence that you've passed your General test.

If you are licensed and already have a call sign, you can begin using your new privileges immediately. When you give your call sign, append "/AG" (on CW or digital modes) or "temporary AG" (on phone). As soon as your name and call sign appear in the FCC's database of licensees, typically a week to 10 days later, you can stop adding the suffix. The CSCE is good for 365 days in case there's a delay or problem with license processing or you decide to upgrade to Extra class before receiving your paper license.

If you don't pass, don't be discouraged! You might be able to take another version of the test right then and there if the session organizers can accommodate you. Even if you decide to try again later, you now know just how the test session feels — you'll be more relaxed and ready next time. The ham bands are full of hams who took their General test more than once before passing. You'll be in good company!

## FCC and ARRL/VEC Licensing Resources

After you pass your exam, the examiners will file all of the necessary paperwork so that your license will be granted by the Federal Communications Commission (FCC). In a few days, you will see your new call sign in the FCC's database via the ARRL's website and later, you'll receive a paper license by mail.

When you passed your Technician exam, you may have applied for your FCC Federal Registration Number (FRN). This allows you to access the information for any FCC licenses you may have and to request modifications to them. These functions are available via the FCC's Universal Licensing System website (**www.fcc.gov/wireless/systems-utilities/universal-licensing-system**) and complete instructions for using the site are available at **www.arrl.org/universal-licensing-system**.

The ARRL/VEC can also process license renewals and modifications for you as described at **www.arrl.org/call-sign-renewals-or-changes**.

# Books to Help
## You Learn

As you study the material on the licensing exam, you will have lots of other questions about the how and why of Amateur Radio. The following references, available from your local bookstore or the ARRL (**www.arrl.org/shop**) will help "fill in the blanks" and give you a broader picture of the hobby:

- *Ham Radio for Dummies*, 3rd edition, by Ward Silver, NØAX. Written for new Technician and General class licensees, this book supplements the information in study guides with an informal, friendly approach to the hobby.

- *ARRL Operating Manual.* With in-depth sections on the most popular ham radio activities, this is your guide to digital mode operating, radiosport, award programs, DXing and more.

- *Understanding Basic Electronics* by Walter Banzhaf, WB1ANE. Students who want more technical background about electronics should take a look at this book. It covers the fundamentals of electricity and electronics that are the foundation of all radio.

- *Basic Radio* by Joel Hallas, W1ZR. Students who want more technical background about radio theory should take a look at this book. It covers the key building blocks of receivers, transmitters, antennas, and propagation.

- *ARRL Handbook.* This is the grandfather of all Amateur Radio references and belongs on the shelf of hams. Almost any topic you can think of in Amateur Radio technology is represented here.

- *ARRL Antenna Book.* After the radio itself, all radio depends on antennas. This book provides information on every common type of amateur antenna, feed lines and related topics, and practical construction tips and techniques.

### Time to Get Started

By following these instructions and carefully studying the material in this book, soon you'll be joining the rest of the General and Extra class licensees on the HF bands! Each of us at the ARRL Headquarters and every ARRL member looks forward to the day when you join the fun. 73 (best regards) and good luck!

# About the ARRL

The seed for Amateur Radio was planted in the 1890s, when Guglielmo Marconi began his experiments in wireless telegraphy. Soon he was joined by dozens, then hundreds, of others who were enthusiastic about sending and receiving messages through the air — some with a commercial interest, but others solely out of a love for this new communications medium. The United States government began licensing Amateur Radio operators in 1912.

By 1914, there were thousands of Amateur Radio operators — hams — in the United States. Hiram Percy Maxim, a leading Hartford, Connecticut inventor and industrialist, saw the need for an organization to unify this fledgling group of radio experimenters. In May 1914 he founded the American Radio Relay League (ARRL) to meet that need.

ARRL is the national association for Amateur Radio in the US. ARRL numbers within its ranks the vast majority of active radio amateurs in the nation and has a proud history of achievement as the standard-bearer in amateur affairs. ARRL's underpinnings as Amateur Radio's witness, partner, and forum are defined by five pillars: Public Service, Advocacy, Education, Technology, and Membership. ARRL is also International Secretariat for the International Amateur Radio Union, which is made up of similar societies in 150 countries around the world.

**ARRL's Mission Statement:** To advance the art, science, and enjoyment of Amateur Radio.
**ARRL's Vision Statement:** As the national association for Amateur Radio in the United States, ARRL:

- Supports the awareness and growth of Amateur Radio worldwide;
- Advocates for meaningful access to radio spectrum;
- Strives for every member to get involved, get active, and get on the air;
- Encourages radio experimentation and, through its members, advances radio technology and education;
  and
- Organizes and trains volunteers to serve their communities by providing public service and emergency communications.

At ARRL headquarters in the Hartford, Connecticut suburb of Newington, the staff helps serve the needs of members. ARRL publishes the monthly journal *QST* and an interactive digital version of *QST*, as well as newsletters and many publications covering all aspects of Amateur Radio. Its headquarters station, W1AW, transmits bulletins of interest to radio amateurs and Morse code practice sessions. ARRL also coordinates an extensive field organization, which includes volunteers who provide technical information and other support services for radio amateurs as well as communications for public service activities. In addition, ARRL represents US radio amateurs to the Federal Communications Commission and other government agencies in the US and abroad.

Membership in ARRL means much more than receiving *QST* each month. In addition to the services already described, ARRL offers membership services on a personal level, such as the Technical Information Service, where members can get answers — by phone, e-mail, or the ARRL website — to all their technical and operating questions.

A bona fide interest in Amateur Radio is the only essential qualification of membership; an Amateur Radio license is not a prerequisite, although full voting membership is granted only to licensed radio amateurs in the US. Full ARRL membership gives you a voice in how the affairs of the organization are governed. ARRL policy is set by a Board of Directors (one from each of 15 Divisions). Each year, one-third of the ARRL Board of Directors stands for election by the full members they represent. The day-to-day operation of ARRL HQ is managed by a Chief Executive Officer and his/her staff.

**Join ARRL Today!** No matter what aspect of Amateur Radio attracts you, ARRL membership is relevant and important. There would be no Amateur Radio as we know it today were it not for ARRL. We would be happy to welcome you as a member! Join online at **www.arrl.org/join**. For more information about ARRL and answers to any questions you may have about Amateur Radio, write or call:

**ARRL — The national association for Amateur Radio®**

225 Main Street
Newington CT 06111-1494
Tel: 860-594-0200
FAX: 860-594-0259
e-mail: **hq@arrl.org**
**www.arrl.org**

Prospective new radio amateurs call (toll-free):
**800-32-NEW HAM (800-326-3942)**
You can also contact ARRL via e-mail at **newham@arrl.org**
or check out the ARRL website at **www.arrl.org**

# ARRL Members
# Get it All!

## Members-Only Web Services

### ▪ QST Digital Edition
In addition to the printed copy of *QST*, all members have access to the online, monthly digital version at no additional cost. *QST* apps are also available.

### ▪ Archives
ARRL members can browse ARRL's extensive online *QST* archive, including downloading and viewing *QST* product reviews. *QST* Product Reviews help our members make smarter, more informed purchasing decisions for Amateur Radio equipment.

### ▪ E-Mail Forwarding Service
E-mail sent to your arrl.net address will be forwarded to any e-mail account you specify.

### ▪ E-Newsletters
Subscribe to the weekly ARRL Letter and a variety of other e-newsletters and announcements: ham radio news, radio clubs, public service, contesting and more!

# Membership Application

## ☑ Membership options (circle your choice)

| | 1 Year | 2 Years | 3 Years | |
|---|---|---|---|---|
| US | $49 | $95 | $140 | Monthly *QST* via standard mail for US members |

Additional membership options are available at www.arrl.org/join. Membership includes $21 per year for subscription to *QST*. Dues subject to change without notice and are nonrefundable.

Name _____  Call Sign _____

Street _____  City _____ State _____ ZIP _____

E-mail _____  Phone _____ Date of Birth _____

Family Member Name _____  Call Sign (if any) _____

## ☑ Payment Options
☐ Total enclosed payable to ARRL $_____

☐ Visa  ☐ MasterCard  ☐ Amex  ☐ Discover  ☐ Check Enclosed

☐ I do not want my name and address made available for non-ARRL related mailings.

Card Number _____  Expiration Date _____

Cardholder's Signature _____

**ARRL, 225 Main St.**
**Newington, CT 06111**    1-888-277-5289    www.arrl.org/join

GCLM 2019

# General Class (Element 3) Syllabus

**Effective July 1, 2019 to June 30, 2023**
## SUBELEMENT G1 — COMMISSION'S RULES
### [5 Exam Questions — 5 Groups] 64 Questions

G1A — General class control operator frequency privileges; primary and secondary allocations

G1B — Antenna structure limitations; good engineering and good amateur practice; beacon operation; prohibited transmissions; retransmitting radio signals

G1C — Transmitter power regulations; data emission standards; 60-meter operation requirements

G1D — Volunteer Examiners and Volunteer Examiner Coordinators; temporary identification; element credit

G1E — Control categories; repeater regulations; third-party rules; ITU regions; automatically controlled digital station

## SUBELEMENT G2 — OPERATING PROCEDURES
### [5 Exam Questions — 5 Groups] 60 Questions

G2A — Phone operating procedures; USB/LSB conventions; breaking into a contact; VOX operation

G2B — Operating courtesy; band plans; emergencies, including drills and emergency communications

G2C — CW operating procedures and procedural signals; Q signals and common abbreviations; full break-in

G2D — Volunteer Monitoring Program; HF operations

G2E — Digital operating procedures

## SUBELEMENT G3 — RADIO WAVE PROPAGATION
### [3 Exam Questions — 3 Groups] 36 Questions

G3A — Sunspots and solar radiation; ionospheric disturbances; propagation forecasting and indices

G3B — Maximum Usable Frequency; Lowest Usable Frequency; propagation

G3C — Ionospheric layers; critical angle and frequency; HF scatter; Near Vertical Incidence Skywave

## SUBELEMENT G4 — AMATEUR RADIO PRACTICES
### [5 Exam Questions — 5 groups] 67 Questions

G4A — Station operation and setup

G4B — Test and monitoring equipment; two-tone test

G4C — Interference to consumer electronics; grounding; DSP

G4D — Speech processors; S meters; sideband operation near band edges

G4E — HF mobile radio installations; alternative energy source operation

## SUBELEMENT G5 — ELECTRICAL PRINCIPLES
### [3 Exam Questions — 3 Groups] 43 Questions

G5A — Reactance; inductance; capacitance; impedance; impedance matching

G5B — The decibel; current and voltage dividers; electrical power calculations; sine wave root-mean-square (RMS) values; PEP calculations

G5C — Resistors, capacitors, and inductors in series and parallel; transformers

## SUBELEMENT G6 — CIRCUIT COMPONENTS
### [2 Exam Questions — 2 Groups] 27 Questions

G6A — Resistors; capacitors; inductors; rectifiers; solid-state diodes and transistors; vacuum tubes; batteries

G6B — Analog and digital integrated circuits (ICs); microprocessors; memory; I/O devices; microwave ICs (MMICs); display devices; connectors; ferrite cores

## SUBELEMENT G7 — PRACTICAL CIRCUITS
### [3 Exam Questions — 3 Groups] 40 Questions

G7A — Power supplies; schematic symbols

G7B — Digital circuits; amplifiers and oscillators

G7C — Receivers and transmitters; filters; oscillators

## SUBELEMENT G8 — SIGNALS AND EMISSIONS
### [3 Exam Questions — 3 Groups] 38 Questions

G8A — Carriers and modulation: AM; FM; single sideband; modulation envelope; digital modulation; overmodulation

G8B — Frequency mixing; multiplication; bandwidths of various modes; deviation; duty cycle; intermodulation

G8C — Digital emission modes

## SUBELEMENT G9 — ANTENNAS AND FEED LINES
### [4 Exam Questions — 4 Groups] 54 Questions

G9A — Antenna feed lines: characteristic impedance and attenuation; SWR calculation, measurement, and effects; matching networks

G9B — Basic antennas

G9C — Directional antennas

G9D — Specialized antennas

## SUBELEMENT G0 — ELECTRICAL AND RF SAFETY
### [2 Exam Questions — 2 Groups] 25 Questions

G0A — RF safety principles, rules and guidelines; routine station evaluation

G0B — Station safety: electrical shock, safety grounding, fusing, interlocks, wiring, antenna and tower safety

# Commission's Rules

Your General class exam (Element 3) will consist of 35 questions taken from the General class question pool as prepared by the Volunteer Examiner Coordinators' Question Pool Committee. A certain number of questions are taken from each of the 10 subelements. There will be 5 questions from the subelement shown in this chapter. These questions are divided into 5 groups, labeled G1A through G1E.

The correct answer (A, B, C, or D) is given in bold at the beginning of an explanation section that follows the question and the possible responses. This convention will be used throughout this book. In addition, at the end of each explanation you'll find the page number where this question is discussed in ARRL's *General Class License Manual*, like this: [*General Class License Manual*, page 3-8].

You'll often see a reference to Part 97 of the Federal Communications Commission rules set in brackets, like this: [97.3(a)(4)]. This tells you where to find the exact wording of the Rules as they relate to that question. You'll find the complete Part 97 Rules on the ARRL website at **www.arrl.org/part-97-amateur-radio**.

## SUBELEMENT G1 — COMMISSION'S RULES
### [5 Exam Questions — 5 Groups]

## G1A — General class control operator frequency privileges; primary and secondary allocations

**G1A01** On which HF/MF bands is a General class license holder granted all amateur frequency privileges?
- A. 60 meters, 20 meters, 17 meters, and 12 meters
- B. 160 meters, 80 meters, 40 meters, and 10 meters
- C. 160 meters, 60 meters, 30 meters, 17 meters, 12 meters, and 10 meters
- D. 160 meters, 30 meters, 17 meters, 15 meters, 12 meters, and 10 meters

**(C)** These are the bands on which the entire range of mode-restricted segments (such as phone or CW/data) are open to all license classes that have access to the band. General, Advanced, and Extra class licensees all have access to the entire band. [97.301(d)] [*General Class License Manual*, page 3-8]

### G1A02 On which of the following bands is phone operation prohibited?

A. 160 meters
B. 30 meters
C. 17 meters
D. 12 meters

**(B)** The 30 meter band is restricted to CW, RTTY, and data transmissions only. Image transmission is also prohibited on the 60 meter band. [97.305] [*General Class License Manual*, page 3-8]

### G1A03 On which of the following bands is image transmission prohibited?

A. 160 meters
B. 30 meters
C. 20 meters
D. 12 meters

**(B)** See G1A02. [97.305] [*General Class License Manual*, page 3-8]

### G1A04 Which of the following amateur bands is restricted to communication only on specific channels, rather than frequency ranges?

A. 11 meters
B. 12 meters
C. 30 meters
D. 60 meters

**(D)** In the US, Amateur Radio is a secondary service to government stations on 60 meters. By limiting amateur operation to specific channels, it is easier for hams to tell when government stations are present and to avoid interfering with them. [97.303 (h)] [*General Class License Manual*, page 3-8]

### G1A05 Which of the following frequencies is in the General class portion of the 40-meter band (in ITU Region 2)?

A. 7.250 MHz
B. 7.500 MHz
C. 40.200 MHz
D. 40.500 MHz

**(A)** General class licensees have access to the following portions of the 40 meter band (f = 300 / 40 = 7.5 MHz): 7.025 – 7.125 MHz on CW/RTTY/Data and from 7.175 – 7.300 MHz on CW/Phone/Image. [97.301(d)] [*General Class License Manual*, page 3-8]

**G1A06** **Which of the following frequencies is within the General class portion of the 75-meter phone band?**

A. 1875 kHz
B. 3750 kHz
C. 3900 kHz
D. 4005 kHz

**(C)** Although the 75 and 80 meter bands are part of a single amateur band, the difference in wavelength is enough for there to be a distinction between 75 meters at the higher frequencies and 80 meters at the lower frequencies. General class licensees have access to the following portions of the 75 meter band (f = 300 / 75 = 4.0 MHz): 3.800 – 4.000 MHz on CW/Phone/Image. [97.301(d)] [*General Class License Manual*, page 3-8]

**G1A07** **Which of the following frequencies is within the General class portion of the 20-meter phone band?**

A. 14005 kHz
B. 14105 kHz
C. 14305 kHz
D. 14405 kHz

**(C)** General class licensees have access to the following portions of the 20 meter band (f = 300 / 20 = 15 MHz): 14.025 – 14.150 MHz on CW/RTTY/ Data and from 14.225 – 14.350 MHz on CW/Phone/Image. [97.301(d)] [*General Class License Manual*, page 3-8]

**G1A08** **Which of the following frequencies is within the General class portion of the 80-meter band?**

A. 1855 kHz
B. 2560 kHz
C. 3560 kHz
D. 3650 kHz

**(C)** See G1A06. General class licensees have access to the following portions of the 80 meter band (f = 300 / 80 = 3.75 MHz): 3.525 – 3.600 MHz on CW/ RTTY/Data. [97.301(d)] [*General Class License Manual*, page 3-8]

**G1A09**　Which of the following frequencies is within the General class portion of the 15-meter band?

A.　14250 kHz
B.　18155 kHz
C.　21300 kHz
D.　24900 kHz

**(C)**　General class licensees have access to the following portions of the 15 meter band (f = 300 / 15 = 20 MHz): 21.025 – 21.200 MHz on CW/RTTY/ Data and from 21.275 – 21.450 MHz on CW/Phone/Image. [97.301(d)] [*General Class License Manual*, page 3-8]

**G1A10**　Which of the following frequencies is available to a control operator holding a General class license?

A.　28.020 MHz
B.　28.350 MHz
C.　28.550 MHz
D.　All these choices are correct

**(D)**　The 28 MHz (10 meter) band is one of the bands on which all mode-restricted segments (such as phone or CW/data) are open to all license classes that have access to the band. Generals, Advanced, and Extra class licensees all have access to the entire band. [97.301(d)] [*General Class License Manual*, page 3-8]

**G1A11**　When General class licensees are not permitted to use the entire voice portion of a band, which portion of the voice segment is generally available to them?

A.　The lower frequency end
B.　The upper frequency end
C.　The lower frequency end on frequencies below 7.3 MHz, and the upper end on frequencies above 14.150 MHz
D.　The upper frequency end on frequencies below 7.3 MHz, and the lower end on frequencies above 14.150 MHz

**(B)**　If you look at the US Amateur Band chart available in the *General Class License Manual* or on the ARRL website at **www.arrl.org/graphical-frequency-allocations** you will see that in the bands on which there are mode-restricted segments, such as 80 meters, General class licensees have access to the higher frequencies of the segment. [97.301] [*General Class License Manual*, page 3-8]

**G1A12**  **Which of the following applies when the FCC rules designate the Amateur Service as a secondary user on a band?**

A. Amateur stations must record the call sign of the primary service station before operating on a frequency assigned to that station
B. Amateur stations can use the band only during emergencies
C. Amateur stations can use the band only if they do not cause harmful interference to primary users
D. Amateur stations may only operate during specific hours of the day, while primary users are permitted 24-hour use of the band

**(C)**　You should always listen before you transmit. This is especially important on bands where Amateur Radio is a secondary service, such as the 30 or 60 meter band. Amateurs are only permitted to use these frequencies if they do not cause harmful interference to the primary users. If you hear a station in the primary service or receive interference from such a station you should immediately change frequencies. Otherwise you might be causing interference to the primary station. [97.303] [*General Class License Manual*, page 3-8]

**G1A13**  **What is the appropriate action if, when operating on either the 30-meter or 60-meter bands, a station in the primary service interferes with your contact?**

A. Notify the FCCs regional Engineer in Charge of the interference
B. Increase your transmitter's power to overcome the interference
C. Attempt to contact the station and request that it stop the interference
D. Move to a clear frequency or stop transmitting

**(D)**　See G1A12. [97.303(h)(2)(j)] [*General Class License Manual*, page 3-8]

**G1A14**  **Which of the following may apply in areas under FCC jurisdiction outside of ITU Region 2?**

A. Station identification may have to be in a language other than English
B. Morse code may not be permitted
C. Digital transmission may not be permitted
D. Frequency allocations may differ

D　There are some areas outside ITU Region 2 where the FCC has jurisdiction. For example, some US-administered Pacific islands (American Samoa, the Northern Mariana Islands, Guam and Wake Island) are in Region 3. In these areas, the FCC frequency rules may be different from those here in Region 2. [97.301(d)] [*General Class License Manual*, page 3-2]

**G1A15** What portion of the 10-meter band is available for repeater use?

A. The entire band
B. The portion between 28.1 MHz and 28.2 MHz
C. The portion between 28.3 MHz and 28.5 MHz
D. The portion above 29.5 MHz

**(D)** Repeaters are allowed above 29.5 MHz. You can download your own copy of amateur frequency allocations from **www.arrl.org/graphical-frequency-allocations**. [97.205(b)] [*General Class License Manual*, page 3-9]

## G1B — Antenna structure limitations; good engineering and good amateur practice; beacon operation; prohibited transmissions; retransmitting radio signals

**G1B01** What is the maximum height above ground to which an antenna structure may be erected without requiring notification to the FAA and registration with the FCC, provided it is not at or near a public use airport?

A. 50 feet
B. 100 feet
C. 200 feet
D. 300 feet

**(C)** FCC regulations require approval if your antenna would be more than 200 feet above ground level. This includes the antenna, the supports and anything else attached to the structure. (Additional FCC restrictions apply if the antenna is within about 4 miles of a public use airport or heliport.) [97.15(a)] [*General Class License Manual*, page 3-3]

**G1B02** With which of the following conditions must beacon stations comply?

A. A beacon station may not use automatic control
B. The frequency must be coordinated with the National Beacon Organization
C. The frequency must be posted on the internet or published in a national periodical
D. There must be no more than one beacon signal transmitting in the same band from the same station location

**(D)** A beacon station normally transmits a signal for operators to observe propagation and reception characteristics. For this purpose, FCC rules specifically allow an amateur beacon to transmit one-way communications. [97.203(b)] [*General Class License Manual*, page 3-10]

**G1B03** **Which of the following is a purpose of a beacon station as identified in the FCC rules?**

A. Observation of propagation and reception
B. Automatic identification of repeaters
C. Transmission of bulletins of general interest to Amateur Radio licensees
D. Identifying net frequencies

**(A)** See G1B02. [97.3(a)(9)] [*General Class License Manual*, page 3-10]

**G1B04** **Which of the following transmissions is permitted?**

A. Unidentified transmissions for test purposes only
B. Retransmission of other amateur station signals by any amateur station
C. Occasional retransmission of weather and propagation forecast information from U.S. government stations
D. Coded messages of any kind, if not intended to facilitate a criminal act

**(C)** In general, you can't retransmit a broadcast but there are exceptions. Broadcasts of weather or propagation predictions from a US government station may be retransmitted, as long as you only do it occasionally. [97.113(c)] [*General Class License Manual*, page 3-13]

**G1B05** **Which of the following one-way transmissions are permitted?**

A. Unidentified test transmissions of less than one minute in duration
B. Transmissions necessary to assist learning the International Morse code
C. Regular transmissions offering equipment for sale, if intended for Amateur Radio use
D. All these choices are correct

**(B)** Generally, one-way transmissions are not permitted but there is an exception for "code practice." [97.111((5)(b)] [*General Class License Manual*, page 3-13]

**G1B06** Under what conditions are state and local governments permitted to regulate Amateur Radio antenna structures?

A. Under no circumstances, FCC rules take priority
B. At any time and to any extent necessary to accomplish a legitimate purpose of the state or local entity, provided that proper filings are made with the FCC
C. Only when such structures exceed 50 feet in height and are clearly visible 1000 feet from the structure
D. Amateur Service communications must be reasonably accommodated, and regulations must constitute the minimum practical to accommodate a legitimate purpose of the state or local entity

**(D)** Local building rules and codes may also affect your ability to put up towers and antennas. In the FCC rule known as PRB-1, the FCC requires that Amateur Service communications must be reasonably accommodated. Any regulations must be the minimum practical and have a legitimate purpose. [97.15(b), PRB-1, 101 FCC 2d 952 (1985)] [*General Class License Manual*, page 3-3]

**G1B07** What are the restrictions on the use of abbreviations or procedural signals in the Amateur Service?

A. Only "Q" signals are permitted
B. They may be used if they do not obscure the meaning of a message
C. They are not permitted
D. Only "10 codes" are permitted

**(B)** The use of common abbreviations and procedural signals is standard practice and does not obscure the meaning of a message because their meaning is well known. Any use of abbreviations or codes for the purpose of obscuring the meaning of a communication is prohibited. [97.113(a)(4)] [*General Class License Manual*, page 3-13]

**G1B08** When choosing a transmitting frequency, what should you do to comply with good amateur practice?

A. Ensure that the frequency and mode selected are within your license class privileges
B. Follow generally accepted band plans agreed to by the Amateur Radio community
C. Monitor the frequency before transmitting
D. All these choices are correct

**(D)** Choosing a frequency is straightforward: Be sure the frequency is authorized to General class licensees, follow the band plan under normal circumstances, and listen on that frequency to avoid interfering with ongoing communications. [97.101(a)] [*General Class License Manual*, page 2-4]

### G1B09 On what HF frequencies are automatically controlled beacons permitted?

A. On any frequency if power is less than 1 watt
B. On any frequency if transmissions are in Morse code
C. 21.08 MHz to 21.09 MHz
D. 28.20 MHz to 28.30 MHz

**(D)** 28.2 to 28.3 MHz is the only HF band segment where beacon operation is authorized by the FCC rules. [97.203(d)] [*General Class License Manual*, page 3-10]

### G1B10 What is the power limit for beacon stations?

A. 10 watts PEP output
B. 20 watts PEP output
C. 100 watts PEP output
D. 200 watts PEP output

**(C)** 100 watts of output power is a good compromise, enabling a beacon station to transmit a signal strong enough to be heard when propagation isn't the best. Similarly, when propagation is good, a 100-watt signal is not so strong as to cause interference to stations on nearby frequencies. [97.203(c)] [*General Class License Manual*, page 3-10]

### G1B11 Who or what determines "good engineering and good amateur practice," as applied to the operation of an amateur station in all respects not covered by the Part 97 rules?

A. The FCC
B. The control operator
C. The IEEE
D. The ITU

**(A)** The FCC does not publish a list of what constitutes "good engineering and good amateur practice" because the state of the radio art is continually improving. Nevertheless, when questions arise, the FCC is the agency that determines what standards should be applied. [97.101(a)] [*General Class License Manual*, page 3-14]

**G1B12** When is it permissible to communicate with amateur stations in countries outside the areas administered by the Federal Communications Commission?

A. Only when the foreign country has a formal third-party agreement filed with the FCC
B. When the contact is with amateurs in any country except those whose administrations have notified the ITU that they object to such communications
C. When the contact is with amateurs in any country as long as the communication is conducted in English
D. Only when the foreign country is a member of the International Amateur Radio Union

**(B)** US amateurs are permitted to communicate with any other country. There have been a very few instances in which a government has prohibited communication between its amateurs and those of another country. [97.111(a)(1)] [*General Class License Manual*, page 3-13]

## G1C — Transmitter power regulations; data emission standards; 60-meter operation requirements

**G1C01** What is the maximum transmitting power an amateur station may use on 10.140 MHz?

A. 200 watts PEP output
B. 1000 watts PEP output
C. 1500 watts PEP output
D. 2000 watts PEP output

**(A)** The general rule is that maximum power is limited to 1500 watts PEP output, although there are exceptions where less power is allowed. One such exception is the 30 meter band, 10.100 – 10.150 MHz, where the maximum power output for US amateurs is 200 watts. [97.313(c)(1)] [*General Class License Manual*, page 3-15]

**G1C02** What is the maximum transmitting power an amateur station may use on the 12-meter band?

A. 50 watts PEP output
B. 200 watts PEP output
C. 1500 watts PEP output
D. An effective radiated power equivalent to 100 watts from a half-wave dipole

**(C)** The maximum power allowed is 1500 watts PEP output from 24.890 – 24.990 MHz. See also G1C01. [97.313(a),(b)] [*General Class License Manual*, page 3-14]

**G1C03** **What is the maximum bandwidth permitted by FCC rules for Amateur Radio stations transmitting on USB frequencies in the 60-meter band?**

A. 2.8 kHz
B. 5.6 kHz
C. 1.8 kHz
D. 3 kHz

**(A)** The FCC Rules for operating on the amateur 60 meter band tell us that "Amateur stations must ensure that their transmission occupies only the 2.8 kHz centered around each" of the operating channels. That means the maximum transmitted bandwidth of an upper sideband signal is 2.8 kHz. A properly adjusted SSB transmitter normally has a bandwidth of 2.5 to 2.8 kHz. This bandwidth limitation also applies to digital signals being transmitted on the 60 meter band. [97.303(h)(1)] [*General Class License Manual*, page 3-15]

**G1C04** **Which of the following limitations apply to transmitter power on every amateur band?**

A. Only the minimum power necessary to carry out the desired communications should be used
B. Power must be limited to 200 watts when using data transmissions
C. Power should be limited as necessary to avoid interference to another radio service on the frequency
D. Effective radiated power cannot exceed 1500 watts

**(A)** Although the maximum power allowed is 1500 watts PEP output, amateurs should use only the power level needed to carry out communications. [97.313(a)] [*General Class License Manual*, page 3-15]

**G1C05** **What is the limit for transmitter power on the 28 MHz band for a General Class control operator?**

A. 100 watts PEP output
B. 1000 watts PEP output
C. 1500 watts PEP output
D. 2000 watts PEP output

**(C)** The maximum power allowed is 1500 watts PEP output on the entire band. See also G1C01. [97.313] [*General Class License Manual*, page 3-15]

**G1C06**    **What is the limit for transmitter power on the 1.8 MHz band?**

A.  200 watts PEP output
B.  1000 watts PEP output
C.  1200 watts PEP output
D.  1500 watts PEP output

**(D)**    The maximum power allowed is 1500 watts PEP output on the entire band. See also G1C01. [97.313] [*General Class License Manual*, page 3-14]

**G1C07**    **What is the maximum symbol rate permitted for RTTY or data emission transmission on the 20-meter band?**

A.  56 kilobaud
B.  19.6 kilobaud
C.  1200 baud
D.  300 baud

**(D)**    The symbol rate of digital signals is restricted to make sure they do not consume too much bandwidth at the expense of other modes. **Table G1.1** shows the limits by band. At the time this book was written in early 2019, the FCC was considering changes to these regulations. Watch for bulletins from the ARRL and other organizations for changes affecting questions G1C07 through G1C11. [97.305(c), 97.307(f)(3)] [*General Class License Manual*, page 3-16]

**G1C08**    **What is the maximum symbol rate permitted for RTTY or data emission transmitted at frequencies below 28 MHz?**

A.  56 kilobaud
B.  19.6 kilobaud
C.  1200 baud
D.  300 baud

**(D)**    See G1C07. [97.307(f)(3)] [*General Class License Manual*, page 3-16]

### Table G1.1
### Maximum Symbol Rates and Bandwidth

| Band | Symbol Rate (baud) | Bandwidth (kHz) |
| --- | --- | --- |
| 160 through 10 m | 300 | 1 |
| 10 m | 1200 | 1 |
| 6 m, 2 m | 19.6k | 20 |
| 1.25 m, 70 cm | 56k | 100 |
| 33 cm and above | no limit | entire band |

**G1C09** **What is the maximum symbol rate permitted for RTTY or data emission transmitted on the 1.25-meter and 70-centimeter bands?**

A. 56 kilobaud
B. 19.6 kilobaud
C. 1200 baud
D. 300 baud

**(A)** See G1C07. [97.305(c), 97.307(f)(5)] [*General Class License Manual*, page 3-16]


**G1C10** **What is the maximum symbol rate permitted for RTTY or data emission transmissions on the 10-meter band?**

A. 56 kilobaud
B. 19.6 kilobaud
C. 1200 baud
D. 300 baud

**(C)** See G1C07. [97.305(c), 97.307(f)(4)] [*General Class License Manual*, page 3-16]


**G1C11** **What is the maximum symbol rate permitted for RTTY or data emission transmissions on the 2-meter band?**

A. 56 kilobaud
B. 19.6 kilobaud
C. 1200 baud
D. 300 baud

**(B)** See G1C07. [97.305(c), 97.307(f)(5)] [*General Class License Manual*, page 3-16]

**G1C12** **Which of the following is required by the FCC rules when operating in the 60-meter band?**

A. If you are using an antenna other than a dipole, you must keep a record of the gain of your antenna

B. You must keep a record of the date, time, frequency, power level, and stations worked

C. You must keep a record of all third-party traffic

D. You must keep a record of the manufacturer of your equipment and the antenna used

**(A)** The FCC Rules for operating on the amateur 60 meter band are quite different from the rules for any other amateur band. One significant difference is the requirement to transmit with no more than 100 watts effective radiated power (ERP). ERP is a measurement of power as compared to that radiated from a dipole. If you are using a half-wavelength dipole antenna, you can use up to 100 W PEP from your transmitter on that band. If you are using an antenna that has some gain compared to a dipole, then you will have to reduce your transmitter power accordingly. If the antenna has a gain of 3 dBd (3 dB compared to a dipole) then you would have to reduce transmitter power by half (to 50 W PEP). The FCC requires you to keep a record of your antenna gain, if it is more than a dipole. This record can either be from the manufacturer's data, from calculations of the gain or from gain measurements. [97.303(i)] [*General Class License Manual*, page 2-6]

**G1C13** **What must be done before using a new digital protocol on the air?**

A. Type-certify equipment to FCC standards

B. Obtain an experimental license from the FCC

C. Publicly document the technical characteristics of the protocol

D. Submit a rule-making proposal to the FCC describing the codes and methods of the technique

**(C)** The FCC requires the technical characteristics of the protocol be publicly documented before using it on the air. [97.309(a)(4)] [*General Class License Manual*, page 3-16]

**G1C14** **What is the maximum power limit on the 60-meter band?**

A. 1500 watts PEP

B. 10 watts RMS

C. ERP of 100 watts PEP with respect to a dipole

D. ERP of 100 watts PEP with respect to an isotropic antenna

**(C)** Amateurs are restricted to 100 W ERP with respect to a half-wave dipole. (See also G1C03.) [97.313(i)] [*General Class License Manual*, page 3-15]

**G1C15   What measurement is specified by FCC rules that regulate maximum power output?**

A. RMS
B. Average
C. Forward
D. PEP

**(D)**     PEP is the standard power measurement specified in the FCC rules for maximum power. [97.313] [*General Class License Manual*, page 3-14]


## G1D — Volunteer Examiners and Volunteer Examiner Coordinators; temporary identification; element credit

**G1D01   Who may receive partial credit for the elements represented by an expired Amateur Radio license?**

A. Any person who can demonstrate that they once held an FCC-issued General, Advanced, or Amateur Extra class license that was not revoked by the FCC
B. Anyone who held an FCC-issued Amateur Radio license that has been expired for not less than 5 years and not more than 15 years
C. Any person who previously held an amateur license issued by another country, but only if that country has a current reciprocal licensing agreement with the FCC
D. Only persons who once held an FCC issued Novice, Technician, or Technician Plus license

**(A)**     The rules grant "lifetime credit" for passing amateur exam elements 3 and 4. The applicant still has to pass element 2 (the Technician exam) however. [97.501, 97.505(a)] [*General Class License Manual*, page 3-5]


**G1D02   What license examinations may you administer when you are an accredited VE holding a General class operator license?**

A. General and Technician
B. General only
C. Technician only
D. Amateur Extra, General, and Technician

**(C)**     Holders of a General class operator license may only administer examinations for the Technician class license. A General class licensee may participate as a VE in any exam session, but may not be the primary VE administering General or Extra class exams. [97.509(b)(3)(i)] [*General Class License Manual*, page 3-4]

**G1D03** **On which of the following band segments may you operate if you are a Technician class operator and have a Certificate of Successful Completion of Examination (CSCE) for General class privileges?**

A. Only the Technician band segments until your upgrade is posted in the FCC database
B. Only on the Technician band segments until your license arrives in the mail
C. On any General or Technician class band segment
D. On any General or Technician class band segment except 30 meters and 60 meters

**(C)** You may begin using the General class privileges immediately on receiving your CSCE, but you must append the temporary identifier to your call sign as described in the discussion for G1D06. [97.9(b)] [*General Class License Manual*, page 3-5]

**G1D04** **Which of the following is a requirement for administering a Technician class license examination?**

A. At least three General class or higher VEs must observe the examination
B. At least two General class or higher VEs must be present
C. At least two General class or higher VEs must be present, but only one need be Amateur Extra class
D. At least three VEs of Technician class or higher must observe the examination

**(A)** All license exams are administered through the Volunteer Examiner Coordinator (VEC) system. VEs (Volunteer Examiners) must be accredited by a VEC. There must be three VEC-accredited VEs present at every exam session. Technician exams are administered by General class or higher VEs. [97.509(3)(i) (c)] [*General Class License Manual*, page 3-4]

**G1D05** **Which of the following must a person have before they can be an administering VE for a Technician class license examination?**

A. Notification to the FCC that you want to give an examination
B. Receipt of a Certificate of Successful Completion of Examination (CSCE) for General class
C. Possession of a properly obtained telegraphy license
D. An FCC General class or higher license and VEC accreditation

**(D)** All license exams are administered through the Volunteer Examiner Coordinator (VEC) system. VEs (Volunteer Examiners) must be accredited by a VEC. There must be three VEC-accredited VEs present at every exam session. Technician exams are administered by General class or higher VEs. As soon as the FCC issues your General class license (meaning that it has appeared in the FCC database) and you receive your accreditation from a VEC, you can participate in exam sessions for Technician license exams. [97.509(b)(3)(i)] [*General Class License Manual*, page 3-4]

**G1D06** **When must you add the special identifier "AG" after your call sign if you are a Technician class licensee and have a Certificate of Successful Completion of Examination (CSCE) for General class operator privileges, but the FCC has not yet posted your upgrade on its website?**

A. Whenever you operate using General class frequency privileges
B. Whenever you operate on any amateur frequency
C. Whenever you operate using Technician frequency privileges
D. A special identifier is not required if your General class license application has been filed with the FCC

**(A)** You must add a "temporary identifier" to your call sign so that stations receiving your transmissions can verify that you are authorized to transmit on that frequency. If a temporary identifier were not used between the time you pass your exam and the time at which your new privileges appear in the FCC database, it would appear that you were transmitting on a frequency for which you were not authorized. When you upgrade to Extra class, you'll append "temporary AE" to your call sign. [97.119(f)(2)] [*General Class License Manual*, page 3-5]

**G1D07**    **Volunteer Examiners are accredited by what organization?**

A. The Federal Communications Commission
B. The Universal Licensing System
C. A Volunteer Examiner Coordinator
D. The Wireless Telecommunications Bureau

**(C)**    A Volunteer Examiner Coordinator (VEC) organization is responsible for certifying Volunteer Examiners and evaluating the results of all exam sessions administered by them. VECs also process all of the license application paperwork and submit it to the FCC. [97.509(b)(1)] [*General Class License Manual*, page 3-4]

**G1D08**    **Which of the following criteria must be met for a non-U.S. citizen to be an accredited Volunteer Examiner?**

A. The person must be a resident of the U.S. for a minimum of 5 years
B. The person must hold an FCC granted Amateur Radio license of General class or above
C. The person's home citizenship must be in ITU region 2
D. None of these choices is correct; a non-U.S. citizen cannot be a Volunteer Examiner

**(B)**    A VE's citizenship does not matter, only whether the individual has demonstrated adequate knowledge of the US Amateur Service rules by passing the appropriate license exams. [97.509(b)(3)] [*General Class License Manual*, page 3-4]

**G1D09**    **How long is a Certificate of Successful Completion of Examination (CSCE) valid for exam element credit?**

A. 30 days
B. 180 days
C. 365 days
D. For as long as your current license is valid

**(C)**    Although your new license class should appear in the FCC database within a few days of passing your examination, should there be a delay, remember that the CSCE is only good for 365 days. After that time, you'll have to re-take the examination! [97.9(b)] [*General Class License Manual*, page 3-4]

**G1D10** **What is the minimum age that one must be to qualify as an accredited Volunteer Examiner?**

A. 12 years
B. 18 years
C. 21 years
D. There is no age limit

**(B)** 18 years old was determined to be an appropriate age to properly manage an amateur examination session. [97.509(b)(2)] [*General Class License Manual*, page 3-4]

**G1D11** **What is required to obtain a new General Class license after a previously-held license has expired and the two-year grace period has passed?**

A. They must have a letter from the FCC showing they once held an amateur or commercial license
B. There are no requirements other than being able to show a copy of the expired license
C. The applicant must be able to produce a copy of a page from a call book published in the U.S. showing his or her name and address
D. The applicant must pass the current Element 2 exam

**(D)** See G1D01. [97.505] [*General Class License Manual*, page 3-5]

## G1E — Control categories; repeater regulations; third-party rules; ITU regions; automatically controlled digital station

**G1E01** **Which of the following would disqualify a third party from participating in stating a message over an amateur station?**

A. The third party's amateur license has been revoked and not reinstated
B. The third party is not a U.S. citizen
C. The third party is a licensed amateur
D. The third party is speaking in a language other than English

**(A)** Third-party communication is available to anyone except someone with a revoked amateur license from any country. This prevents someone whose ability to make use of Amateur Radio was taken away from regaining access to amateur frequencies under the guise of third-party communications. [97.115(b)(2)] [*General Class License Manual*, page 3-11]

**G1E02** **When may a 10-meter repeater retransmit the 2-meter signal from a station that has a Technician class control operator?**

A. Under no circumstances
B. Only if the station on 10-meters is operating under a Special Temporary Authorization allowing such retransmission
C. Only during an FCC-declared general state of communications emergency
D. Only if the 10-meter repeater control operator holds at least a General class license

**(D)**  FCC rules allow any holder of an amateur license to be the control operator of a repeater. The control operator of the repeater must have privileges on the frequency on which the repeater is transmitting, however. A 10 meter repeater must have a General class or higher control operator because Technician and Novice licensees don't have privileges on the 10 meter repeater band. A 10 meter repeater may retransmit the 2 meter signal from a Technician class operator because the 10 meter control operator holds at least a General class license. [97.205(b)] [*General Class License Manual*, page 3-13]

**G1E03** **What is required to conduct communications with a digital station operating under automatic control outside the automatic control band segments?**

A. The station initiating the contact must be under local or remote control
B. The interrogating transmission must be made by another automatically controlled station
C. No third-party traffic may be transmitted
D. The control operator of the interrogating station must hold an Amateur Extra Class license

**(A)**  A human control operator must initiate and monitor communications with automatically controlled stations in order to prevent interference and insure proper operating practices. [97.221] [*General Class License Manual*, page 6-13]

**G1E04** **Which of the following conditions require a licensed Amateur Radio operator to take specific steps to avoid harmful interference to other users or facilities?**

A. When operating within one mile of an FCC Monitoring Station
B. When using a band where the Amateur Service is secondary
C. When a station is transmitting spread spectrum emissions
D. All these choices are correct

**(D)** Aside from the general requirement to avoid causing harmful interference to other licensed stations and primary service licensees, there are several specific instances in which amateurs must take extra steps to avoid interference. FCC Monitoring Stations require an environment free of strong or spurious signals that can cause interference. The location of monitoring stations can be determined from a regional FCC office. Spread spectrum (SS) transmissions, because of their nature, have the potential to interfere with fixed frequency stations, so SS users should be sure their transmissions will not cause interference. [97.13(b), 97.303, 97.311(b)] [*General Class License Manual*, page 3-8]

**G1E05** **What types of messages for a third party in another country may be transmitted by an amateur station?**

A. Any message, as long as the amateur operator is not paid
B. Only messages for other licensed amateurs
C. Only messages relating to Amateur Radio or remarks of a personal character, or messages relating to emergencies or disaster relief
D. Any messages, as long as the text of the message is recorded in the station log

**(C)** The FCC and other licensing authorities want to be very sure that the amateur service is not abused to provide communications that should properly be conducted through commercial or government services. As a result, third-party communication is restricted to the types of messages in answer C. [97.115(a)(2),97.117] [*General Class License Manual*, page 3-11]

**G1E06** **The frequency allocations of which ITU region apply to radio amateurs operating in North and South America?**

A. Region 4
B. Region 3
C. Region 2
D. Region 1

**(C)** The ITU has created three administrative areas, called *regions*. Each region has its own set of frequency allocations or divisions of the radio spectrum. See **www.iaru.org/regions.html**. North and South America, Alaska, Hawaii, and most US territories and possessions are in Region 2. [97.301, ITU Radio Regulations] [*General Class License Manual*, page 3-2]

**G1E07**    In what part of the 13-centimeter band may an amateur station communicate with non-licensed Wi-Fi stations?

A. Anywhere in the band
B. Channels 1 through 4
C. Channels 42 through 45
D. No part

**(D)**    Even if the station in primary service is using the same type of signal, amateurs in the secondary service may not contact them. [97.111] [*General Class License Manual*, page 3-8]

**G1E08**    What is the maximum PEP output allowed for spread spectrum transmissions?

A. 100 milliwatts
B. 10 watts
C. 100 watts
D. 1500 watts

**(B)**    Since spread spectrum creates a noise-like signal that can affect other users, the output power limit for amateurs for SS signals is 10 watts. [97.313(j)] [*General Class License Manual*, page 3-15]

**G1E09**    Under what circumstances are messages that are sent via digital modes exempt from Part 97 third-party rules that apply to other modes of communication?

A. Under no circumstances
B. When messages are encrypted
C. When messages are not encrypted
D. When under automatic control

**(A)**    Because the messages are transmitted via Amateur Radio they must comply with all amateur rules. This means messages with commercial content or concerning business or pecuniary (financial) interests of the operator may not be transmitted via Amateur Radio. [97.115] [*General Class License Manual*, page 6-14]

**G1E10** **Why should an amateur operator normally avoid transmitting on 14.100, 18.110, 21.150, 24.930 and 28.200 MHz?**

A. A system of propagation beacon stations operates on those frequencies
B. A system of automatic digital stations operates on those frequencies
C. These frequencies are set aside for emergency operations
D. These frequencies are set aside for bulletins from the FCC

**(A)** Amateurs should avoid transmitting on the frequencies of the system of international beacons operated by the Northern California DX Foundation (**www.ncdxf.org/beacon/**). [97.101] [*General Class License Manual*, page 3-10]

**G1E11** **On what bands may automatically controlled stations transmitting RTTY or data emissions communicate with other automatically controlled digital stations?**

A. On any band segment where digital operation is permitted
B. Anywhere in the non-phone segments of the 10-meter or shorter wavelength bands
C. Only in the non-phone Extra Class segments of the bands
D. Anywhere in the 6 meter or shorter wavelength bands, and in limited segments of some of the HF bands

**(D)** Automatically controlled stations respond without a human control operator being present, so the FCC restricts them to certain segments of the amateur HF bands. Automatically controlled stations are permitted to contact other automatically controlled stations anywhere RTTY and data are permitted on the 6-meter and shorter wavelength bands. [97.221, 97.305] [*General Class License Manual*, page 6-13]

# Operating Procedures

Your General class exam (Element 3) will consist of 35 questions taken from the General class question pool as prepared by the Volunteer Examiner Coordinators' Question Pool Committee. A certain number of questions are taken from each of the 10 subelements. There will be 5 questions from the subelement shown in this chapter. These questions are divided into 5 groups, labeled G2A through G2E. There will be five questions from the subelement shown in this chapter.

After some of the explanations in this chapter you will see a reference to Part 97 of the FCC rules set inside square brackets, such as [97.301(d)]. This tells you where to look for the exact wording of the rules as they relate to that question. For a complete copy of Part 97, see the ARRL website, **www.arrl.org/ part-97-amateur-radio**.

## SUBELEMENT G2 — OPERATING PROCEDURES
## [5 Exam Questions — 5 Groups]

### G2A — Phone operating procedures; USB/LSB conventions; breaking into a contact; VOX operation

**G2A01**    **Which sideband is most commonly used for voice communications on frequencies of 14 MHz or higher?**

    A.  Upper sideband
    B.  Lower sideband
    C.  Vestigial sideband
    D.  Double sideband

**(A)**    Single-sideband (SSB) modulation removes the carrier and one sideband from a double-sideband AM signal to conserve spectrum and for improved power efficiency. Amateurs normally use the upper sideband for 20 meter phone operation. Whether the upper or lower sideband is used is strictly a matter of convention and not regulated except on 60 meters where upper sideband is required. The convention to use the lower sideband on the bands below 9 MHz and the upper sideband on the higher-frequency bands developed from the design requirements of early SSB transmitters. Although modern amateur SSB equipment is more flexible, the convention persists. If everyone else on a particular band is using a certain sideband, you will need to use the same one in order to be able to communicate. [*General Class License Manual*, page 2-9]

**G2A02** Which of the following modes is most commonly used for voice communications on the 160-meter, 75-meter, and 40-meter bands?

A. Upper sideband
B. Lower sideband
C. Vestigial sideband
D. Double sideband

**(B)** Amateurs normally use the lower sideband for 160, 75, and 40 meter phone operation. (See also G2A01.) [*General Class License Manual*, page 2-9]

**G2A03** Which of the following is most commonly used for SSB voice communications in the VHF and UHF bands?

A. Upper sideband
B. Lower sideband
C. Vestigial sideband
D. Double sideband

**(A)** Amateurs normally use the upper sideband for VHF and UHF phone operation. (See also G2A01.) [*General Class License Manual*, page 2-9]

**G2A04** Which mode is most commonly used for voice communications on the 17-meter and 12-meter bands?

A. Upper sideband
B. Lower sideband
C. Vestigial sideband
D. Double sideband

**(A)** Amateurs normally use the upper sideband for 17 and 12 meter phone operation. (See also G2A01.) [*General Class License Manual*, page 2-9]

**G2A05**   **Which mode of voice communication is most commonly used on the HF amateur bands?**

A. Frequency modulation
B. Double sideband
C. Single sideband
D. Phase modulation

**(C)**   Most amateurs who use voice communications on the high frequency bands use single sideband (SSB) voice. There are some operators who prefer the high-fidelity sound of double-sideband amplitude modulation (AM). AM requires more than twice the bandwidth of an SSB signal, however. There is also some frequency modulated (FM) and phase modulated (PM) voice operation on the 10 meter band, but that mode also requires a much wider bandwidth than SSB. Some amateurs are beginning to experiment with digitally encoded voice communications, but SSB is the most common HF voice mode. [*General Class License Manual*, page 2-9]

**G2A06**   **Which of the following is an advantage when using single sideband, as compared to other analog voice modes on the HF amateur bands?**

A. Very high fidelity voice modulation
B. Less subject to interference from atmospheric static crashes
C. Ease of tuning on receive and immunity to impulse noise
D. Less bandwidth used and greater power efficiency

**(D)**   Single sideband (SSB) voice communication is used much more frequently than other voice modes on the HF bands because it uses less spectrum space. One sideband and the RF carrier are not transmitted with an SSB signal. That means SSB transmissions are more power efficient, since the full transmitter power is used for the remaining sideband rather than being divided between the two sidebands and carrier as it would be for AM. [*General Class License Manual*, page 2-9]

### G2A07  Which of the following statements is true of the single sideband voice mode?

A. Only one sideband and the carrier are transmitted; the other sideband is suppressed

B. Only one sideband is transmitted; the other sideband and carrier are suppressed

C. SSB is the only voice mode that is authorized on the 20-meter, 15-meter, and 10-meter amateur bands

D. SSB is the only voice mode that is authorized on the 160-meter, 75-meter, and 40-meter amateur bands

**(B)**    Single sideband (SSB) voice transmissions are identified by which sideband is used. If the sideband with a frequency lower than the RF carrier frequency is used, then the signal is known as a lower sideband (LSB) transmission. If the sideband with a frequency higher than the RF carrier frequency is used, then the signal is known as an upper sideband (USB) transmission. In both cases the opposite sideband is suppressed. Amateurs normally use lower sideband on the 160, 75/80, and 40 meter bands, and upper sideband on the 20, 17, 15, 12 and 10 meter bands. This is not a requirement of the FCC Rules in Part 97, though. It is simply by common agreement. FCC Rules do, however, require amateurs to use USB on the five channels of the 60 meter band. [*General Class License Manual*, page 2-9]

### G2A08  What is the recommended way to break in to a phone contact?

A. Say "QRZ" several times followed by your call sign

B. Say your call sign once

C. Say "Breaker Breaker"

D. Say "CQ" followed by the call sign of either station

**(B)**    Breaking into a conversation is easiest if you wait until both stations are listening so that your signal will be heard. In order to identify your transmissions during this brief period, simply state your call sign. No "over" or "break" is required, nor do you have to give either of the transmitting station's call signs. [*General Class License Manual*, page 2-5]

### G2A09  Why do most amateur stations use lower sideband on the 160-meter, 75-meter, and 40-meter bands?

A. Lower sideband is more efficient than upper sideband at these frequencies

B. Lower sideband is the only sideband legal on these frequency bands

C. Because it is fully compatible with an AM detector

D. It is good amateur practice

**(D)**    See G2A02. [*General Class License Manual*, page 2-9]

**G2A10** **Which of the following statements is true of voice VOX operation versus PTT operation?**

A. The received signal is more natural sounding
B. It allows "hands free" operation
C. It occupies less bandwidth
D. It provides more power output

**(B)** The purpose of a voice operated transmit (VOX) circuit is to provide automatic transmit/receive (TR) switching within an amateur station. By simply speaking into the microphone, the antenna is connected to transmitter, the receiver is muted and the transmitter is activated. When you stop speaking, the VOX circuit switches everything back to receive. Using VOX allows hands-free operation since you do not have to press a push-to-talk (PTT) switch. [*General Class License Manual*, page 2-12]

**G2A11** **Generally, who should respond to a station in the contiguous 48 states who calls "CQ DX"?**

A. Any caller is welcome to respond
B. Only stations in Germany
C. Any stations outside the lower 48 states
D. Only contest stations

**(C)** If you hear "CQ DX" from a station on the US mainland, it usually means the CQer is looking for stations outside the lower 48 states. On the HF bands, "DX" generally refers to any station outside the caller's country. [*General Class License Manual*, page 2-5]

**G2A12** **What control is typically adjusted for proper ALC setting on an amateur single sideband transceiver?**

A. The RF clipping level
B. Transmit audio or microphone gain
C. Antenna inductance or capacitance
D. Attenuator level

**(B)** The Automatic Level Control (ALC) circuit in a transceiver reduces microphone gain when it detects excessive power levels at the input to the RF power amplifier stages. For proper adjustment on most transmitters, the microphone gain control should be adjusted so that there is a slight movement of the ALC meter on modulation peaks. [*General Class License Manual*, page 5-11]

## G2B — Operating courtesy; band plans; emergencies, including drills and emergency communications

**G2B01**  Which of the following is true concerning access to frequencies?

A. Nets always have priority
B. QSOs in progress always have priority
C. Except during emergencies, no amateur station has priority access to any frequency
D. Contest operations must always yield to non-contest use of frequencies

**(C)**  Except when the FCC has declared a communications emergency and designated specific frequencies for emergency communications, no single or group of amateurs has priority on any amateur frequency. Good operating practice is to use the flexibility of the amateur service to avoid and minimize interference. [97.101(b), (c)] [*General Class License Manual*, page 2-2]

**G2B02**  What is the first thing you should do if you are communicating with another amateur station and hear a station in distress break in?

A. Continue your communication because you were on the frequency first
B. Acknowledge the station in distress and determine what assistance may be needed
C. Change to a different frequency
D. Immediately cease all transmissions

**(B)**  Whenever you hear a station in distress (where there is immediate threat to human life or property), you should take whatever action is necessary to determine what assistance that station needs and attempt to provide it. Don't assume that some other station will handle the emergency; you may be the only station receiving the distress signal. If you do hear a station in distress, the first thing you should do is to acknowledge that you heard the station, and then ask the operator where they are located and what assistance they need. [*General Class License Manual*, page 2-18]

**G2B03**  **What is good amateur practice if propagation changes during a contact and you notice interference from other stations on the frequency?**

A. Tell the interfering stations to change frequency
B. Report the interference to your local Amateur Auxiliary Coordinator
C. Attempt to resolve the interference problem with the other stations in a mutually acceptable manner
D. Increase power to overcome interference

**(C)** Good operating practice suggests that whoever can most easily resolve an interference problem be the one to do so. If you begin to have interference from other activity on the same frequency, moving your contact to another frequency may be the simplest thing to do. Switching antennas or rotating a beam antenna may also achieve the same results. [*General Class License Manual*, page 2-4]

**G2B04**  **When selecting a CW transmitting frequency, what minimum separation should be used to minimize interference to stations on adjacent frequencies?**

A. 5 to 50 Hz
B. 150 to 500 Hz
C. 1 to 3 kHz
D. 3 to 6 kHz

**(B)** The more bandwidth signals occupy, the more separation is needed between contacts to avoid interference. CW emissions require the least bandwidth and need the least separation. Most radios use narrow filters for CW reception, so you should be able to select an operating frequency within about 150 to 500 Hz from another CW station without causing interference. [*General Class License Manual*, page 2-2]

**G2B05**  **When selecting an SSB transmitting frequency, what minimum separation should be used to minimize interference to stations on adjacent frequencies?**

A. 5 to 50 Hz
B. 150 to 500 Hz
C. Approximately 3 kHz
D. Approximately 6 kHz

**(C)** The more bandwidth signals occupy, the more separation is needed between contacts to avoid interference. Single-sideband (SSB) signals use considerably more bandwidth than CW and therefore need much more separation between contacts. Under normal circumstances, you will need approximately 3 kHz of separation from another contact to avoid causing interference. [*General Class License Manual*, page 2-2]

**G2B06**  **What is a practical way to avoid harmful interference on an apparently clear frequency before calling CQ on CW or phone?**

    A.  Send "QRL?" on CW, followed by your call sign; or, if using phone, ask if the frequency is in use, followed by your call sign

    B.  Listen for 2 minutes before calling CQ

    C.  Send the letter "V" in Morse code several times and listen for a response, or say "test" several times and listen for a response

    D.  Send "QSY" on CW or if using phone, announce "the frequency is in use," then give your call sign and listen for a response

**(A)**    After listening for a short period of time, if you do not hear another station transmitting on the frequency, it is good practice to make a short transmission asking if the frequency is in use. It may be that due to propagation you are unable to hear the transmitting station, but the listening station can hear you. On CQ, the Q signal "QRL?", and on phone, "Is the frequency in use?" followed by your call sign, gives the opportunity for another station to respond. [*General Class License Manual*, page 2-2]

**G2B07**  **Which of the following complies with good amateur practice when choosing a frequency on which to initiate a call?**

    A.  Check to see if the channel is assigned to another station

    B.  Identify your station by transmitting your call sign at least 3 times

    C.  Follow the voluntary band plan for the operating mode you intend to use

    D.  All these choices are correct

**(C)**    Under normal conditions, following the voluntary band plan in **Table G2.1** is a good way to choose a frequency compatible with your planned type of operating. Very crowded bands or special operating events require that you be flexible in your frequency choices. [*General Class License Manual*, page 2-2]

## Table G2.1

## ARRL Considerate Operator's Frequency Guide for HF Bands

*Frequency*      *Mode*

### 160 Meters (1.8 – 2.0 MHz):

| | |
|---|---|
| 1.800 – 2.000 | CW |
| 1.800 – 1.810 | Digital Modes |
| 1.810 | QRP CW calling frequency |
| 1.843 – 2.000 | SSB, SSTV, other wideband modes |
| 1.910 | QRP SSB calling frequency |
| 1.995 – 2.000 | Experimental |
| 1.999 – 2.000 | Beacons |

### 80 Meters (3.5 – 4.0 MHz):

| | |
|---|---|
| 3.500 – 3.510 | CW DX window |
| 3.560 | QRP CW calling frequency |
| 3.570 – 3.600 | RTTY/Data |
| 3.585 – 3.600 | Automatically controlled data stations |
| 3.590 | RTTY/Data DX |
| 3.790 – 3.800 | DX window |
| 3.845 | SSTV |
| 3.885 | AM calling frequency |
| 3.985 | QRP SSB calling frequency |

### 40 Meters (7.0 – 7.3 MHz):

| | |
|---|---|
| 7.030 | QRP CW calling frequency |
| 7.040 | RTTY/Data DX |
| 7.070 – 7.125 | RTTY/Data |
| 7.100 – 7.105 | Automatically controlled data stations |
| 7.171 | SSTV |
| 7.173 | D-SSTV |
| 7.285 | QRP SSB calling frequency |
| 7.290 | AM calling frequency |

### 30 Meters (10.1 – 10.15 MHz):

| | |
|---|---|
| 10.130-10.140 | RTTY/Data |
| 10.140-10.150 | Automatically controlled data stations |

### 20 Meters (14.0 – 14.35 MHz):

| | |
|---|---|
| 14.060 | QRP CW calling frequency |
| 14.070 – 14.095 | RTTY/Data |
| 14.095 – 14.0995 | Automatically controlled data stations |
| 14.100 | IBP/NCDXF Beacons |
| 14.1005 – 14.112 | Automatically controlled data stations |
| 14.230 | SSTV |
| 14.233 | D-SSTV |
| 14.236 | Digital voice |
| 14.285 | QRP SSB calling frequency |
| 14.286 | AM calling frequency |

**17 Meters (18.068 – 18.168 MHz):**

| | |
|---|---|
| 18.100 – 18.105 | RTTY/Data |
| 18.105 – 18.110 | Automatically controlled data stations |
| 18.110 | IBP/NCDXF Beacons |
| 18.162.5 | Digital voice |

**15 Meters (21.0 – 21.45 MHz):**

| | |
|---|---|
| 21.060 | QRP CW calling frequency |
| 21.070 – 21.110 | RTTY/Data |
| 21.090 – 21.100 | Automatically controlled data stations |
| 21.150 | IBP/NCDXF Beacons |
| 21.340 | SSTV |
| 21.385 | QRP SSB calling frequency |

**12 Meters (24.89 – 24.99 MHz):**

| | |
|---|---|
| 24.920 – 24.925 | RTTY/Data |
| 24.925 – 24.930 | Automatically controlled data stations |
| 24.930 | IBP/NCDXF Beacons |

**10 Meters (28 – 29.7 MHz):**

| | |
|---|---|
| 28.060 | QRP CW calling frequency |
| 28.070 – 28.120 | RTTY/Data |
| 28.120 – 28.189 | Automatically controlled data stations |
| 28.190 – 28.225 | Beacons |
| 28.200 | IBP/NCDXF Beacons |
| 28.385 | QRP SSB calling frequency |
| 28.680 | SSTV |
| 29.000-29.200 | AM |
| 29.300-29.510 | Satellite Downlinks |
| 29.520-29.590 | Repeater Inputs |
| 29.600 | FM Simplex |
| 29.610-29.700 | Repeater Outputs |

---

**G2B08** **What is the voluntary band plan restriction for U.S. stations transmitting within the 48 contiguous states in the 50.1 to 50.125 MHz band segment?**

A. Only contacts with stations not within the 48 contiguous states
B. Only contacts with other stations within the 48 contiguous states
C. Only digital contacts
D. Only SSTV contacts

**(A)** DX windows were originally devised to give amateurs from countries with restricted privileges a bit of band space to make DX contacts outside their own country or region. As world-wide frequency allocations become more common, the DX windows are less needed but are still part of operating on some bands. For example, if you live in the US, the DX window of 50.1 to 50.125 MHz is where you listen for and make long-distance contacts with stations outside the contiguous 48 states. [*General Class License Manual*, page 2-5]

**G2B09** **Who may be the control operator of an amateur station transmitting in RACES to assist relief operations during a disaster?**

A. Only a person holding an FCC-issued amateur operator license
B. Only a RACES net control operator
C. A person holding an FCC-issued amateur operator license or an appropriate government official
D. Any control operator when normal communication systems are operational

**(A)** The control operator of a RACES station must have an FCC-issued amateur operator license and be certified by a civil defense organization as a member. [97.407(a)] [*General Class License Manual*, page 2-17]

**G2B10** **When is an amateur station allowed to use any means at its disposal to assist another station in distress?**

A. Only when transmitting in RACES
B. At any time when transmitting in an organized net
C. At any time during an actual emergency
D. Only on authorized HF frequencies

**(C)** No FCC rule prevents an amateur station from using any means of radiocommunications at its disposal to assist a station in distress. [97.405(b)] [*General Class License Manual*, page 2-18]

**G2B11** **What frequency should be used to send a distress call?**

A. Whichever frequency has the best chance of communicating the distress message
B. Only frequencies authorized for RACES or ARES stations
C. Only frequencies that are within your operating privileges
D. Only frequencies used by police, fire, or emergency medical services

**(A)** When normal communications are not available and the immediate safety of human life or protection of property is involved, all of the normal rules for an amateur station are suspended so that you can obtain assistance. This means that any method of communication, on any frequency, and at any power output may be used to communicate and resolve the emergency. It doesn't matter if the distress is personal to the station or a general disaster. Just be sure you have a real emergency! [97.405] [*General Class License Manual*, page 2-18]

# G2C — CW operating procedures and procedural signals; Q signals and common abbreviations; full break-in

**G2C01**     Which of the following describes full break-in telegraphy (QSK)?

A. Breaking stations send the Morse code prosign "BK"
B. Automatic keyers, instead of hand keys, are used to send Morse code
C. An operator must activate a manual send/receive switch before and after every transmission
D. Transmitting stations can receive between code characters and elements

**(D)**     Full break-in telegraphy allows you to receive signals between your transmitted Morse code dots and dashes and between words. The advantage is that if you are making a long transmission, the receiving station can make a short transmission and get your attention. QSK is the Q signal used to describe this type of operation. [*General Class License Manual*, page 2-13]

**G2C02**     What should you do if a CW station sends "QRS?"

A. Send slower
B. Change frequency
C. Increase your power
D. Repeat everything twice

**(A)**     QRS is the Q signal that means "Send slower". To ask if you should send slower, send QRS? Conversely, to increase speed, QRQ is used. [*General Class License Manual*, page 2-13]

**G2C03**     What does it mean when a CW operator sends "KN" at the end of a transmission?

A. Listening for novice stations
B. Operating full break-in
C. Listening only for a specific station or stations
D. Closing station now

**(C)**     $\overline{\text{KN}}$ is an example of a CW prosign, procedural signals that help coordinate the exchange of messages and the beginning and ending of transmissions. The patterns of dots and dashes that make up prosigns are described by a pair of regular letters that, if sent together without a pause, are equivalent to the prosign. (Prosigns are often written with a line over the letters to indicate they are sent with no spaces between them as a single character.) [*General Class License Manual*, page 2-13]

**G2C04    What does the Q signal "QRL?" mean?**

A. "Will you keep the frequency clear?"
B. "Are you operating full break-in?" or "Can you operate full break-in?"
C. "Are you listening only for a specific station?"
D. "Are you busy?" or "Is this frequency in use?"

**(D)**     QRL? is a Q signal hams use most commonly to ask if a frequency is in use before making an initial transmission. [*General Class License Manual*, page 2-2]

**G2C05    What is the best speed to use when answering a CQ in Morse code?**

A. The fastest speed at which you are comfortable copying, but no slower than the CQ
B. The fastest speed at which you are comfortable copying, but no faster than the CQ
C. At the standard calling speed of 10 wpm
D. At the standard calling speed of 5 wpm

**(B)**     An operator calling CQ is assumed to be sending at a speed at which he or she feels comfortable receiving. Responding at a significantly higher speed is impolite and may be embarrassing to the other operator if they are unable to copy your response. If you are uncomfortable responding at the sending station's speed, send at the highest rate at which you are comfortable receiving. It is good practice to respond to calling stations at their sending speed, if it is significantly slower. [*General Class License Manual*, page 2-13]

**G2C06    What does the term "zero beat" mean in CW operation?**

A. Matching the speed of the transmitting station
B. Operating split to avoid interference on frequency
C. Sending without error
D. Matching the transmit frequency to the frequency of a received signal

**(D)**     Zero beat means to match the frequency of the transmitting station. When separate receivers and transmitters were the norm, a transmitter's frequency had to be adjusted to match the received signal's frequency. This was done by spotting — turning on the transmitter's low power stages and listening for that signal in the receiver. When the beat frequency between the desired signal and the transmitter's spotting signal reached zero frequency or zero beat, the transmitter signal and the received signal were on the same frequency. [*General Class License Manual*, page 2-13]

**G2C07**    When sending CW, what does a "C" mean when added to the RST report?

A. Chirpy or unstable signal
B. Report was read from an S meter rather than estimated
C. 100 percent copy
D. Key clicks

**(A)**    An RST with "C" appended, such as 579C, indicates that the signal is being received with chirp, a short frequency shift as the transmitter stabilizes after keying. It's a very distinctive sound and is caused by the transmitter's oscillator changing frequency when the key is closed. Chirp is often the result of low voltage from the power supply or battery. [*General Class License Manual*, page 2-11]

**G2C08**    What prosign is sent to indicate the end of a formal message when using CW?

A. SK
B. BK
C. AR
D. KN

**(C)**    The ARRL National Traffic System has established specific procedures for passing formal written messages by Amateur Radio. Even if you don't participate in traffic nets, it is a good idea to be familiar with the procedures for handling such messages. It can be especially helpful in an emergency for a number of reasons. By following the standard procedures it is more likely that an emergency message will be transmitted (and received) correctly. When sending formal messages using Morse code (CW), you send the message preamble, the address, message body and signature. To indicate that this is the end of the message, send the CW procedural signal (prosign) $\overline{AR}$ to show clearly that all the information has been sent. When the receiving station has accurately recorded the entire message, they will acknowledge receipt of the message by sending "QSL" or simply "R" for "received." (See also G2C03.) [*General Class License Manual*, page 2-13]

**G2C09**    What does the Q signal "QSL" mean?

A. Send slower
B. We have already confirmed by card
C. I acknowledge receipt
D. We have worked before

**(C)**    QSL is the Q signal that means "I acknowledge receipt". Informally, it is often used to indicate that a transmission was received and understood. QSL cards are exchanged to confirm that a contact was made. [*General Class License Manual*, page 2-13]

### G2C10    What does the Q signal "QRN" mean?

A.  Send more slowly
B.  Stop sending
C.  Zero beat my signal
D.  I am troubled by static

**(B)**     QRN is the Q signal that means a station is experiencing interference from atmospheric static or noise. The related Q signal QRM refers to interference from other signals. [*General Class License Manual*, page 2-11]


### G2C11    What does the Q signal "QRV" mean?

A.  You are sending too fast
B.  There is interference on the frequency
C.  I am quitting for the day
D.  I am ready to receive messages

**(D)**     QRV is the Q signal that means "I am ready to copy" and indicates that the station with the message may begin transmitting. QRV is used whether sending formal traffic or having a regular conversation. [*General Class License Manual*, page 2-13]


## G2D — Volunteer Monitoring Program; HF operations

### G2D01    What is the Volunteer Monitoring Program?

A.  Amateur volunteers who are formally enlisted to monitor the airwaves for rules violations
B.  Amateur volunteers who conduct amateur licensing examinations
C.  Amateur volunteers who conduct frequency coordination for amateur VHF repeaters
D.  Amateur volunteers who use their station equipment to help civil defense organizations in times of emergency

**(A)**     The purpose of the Volunteer Monitoring Program is to help ensure amateur self-regulation and see that amateurs follow the FCC rules properly. The Volunteer Monitoring Program volunteers deal only with amateur-to-amateur interference and improper operation. The other answer choices describe other Amateur Radio activities. Amateur volunteers who conduct licensing examinations are called Volunteer Examiners (VEs). Amateurs in charge of frequency coordination for repeaters are called Frequency Coordinators. Amateurs who help civil defense organizations in times of emergency are members of the Radio Amateur Civil Emergency Service (RACES). [*General Class License Manual*, page 3-3]

**G2D02** Which of the following are objectives of the Volunteer Monitoring Program?

A. To conduct efficient and orderly amateur licensing examinations
B. To encourage self-regulation and compliance with the rules by radio amateur operators
C. To coordinate repeaters for efficient and orderly spectrum usage
D. To provide emergency and public safety communications

**(B)** Many amateurs also volunteer to help provide emergency and public safety communications as members of ARRL's Amateur Radio Emergency Service (ARES). (See also G2D01.) [*General Class License Manual*, page 3-2]

**G2D03** What skills learned during hidden transmitter hunts are of help to the Volunteer Monitoring Program?

A. Identification of out of band operation
B. Direction finding used to locate stations violating FCC Rules
C. Identification of different call signs
D. Hunters have an opportunity to transmit on non-amateur frequencies

**(B)** Friendly competitions to locate hidden transmitters, sometimes called "fox hunts" or "bunny hunts," allow participants to practice their radio direction-finding skills which are useful in locating harmful interference sources. The Volunteer Monitoring Program can use "fox hunters" to document interference cases and report them to the proper enforcement bureau. Fox hunts also make everyone aware that there is a plan in place to find and eliminate an interference source [*General Class License Manual*, page 3-3]

**G2D04** Which of the following describes an azimuthal projection map?

A. A map that shows accurate land masses
B. A map that shows true bearings and distances from a particular location
C. A map that shows the angle at which an amateur satellite crosses the equator
D. A map that shows the number of degrees longitude that an amateur satellite appears to move westward at the equator with each orbit

**(B)** An azimuthal map, or azimuthal-equidistant projection map, is also called a great circle map (see **Figure G2.1**). When this type of map is centered on your location, a straight line shows the true direction (bearing) and shortest path to the destination. (The bearing 180 degrees different from the short-path direction shows the direction to point your antenna for long-path communications.) [*General Class License Manual*, page 7-9]

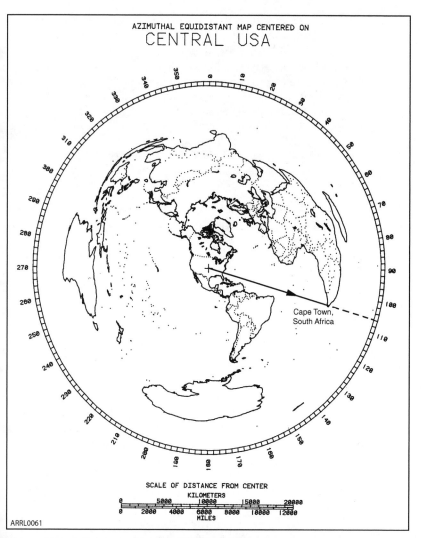

Figure G2.1 — This azimuthal equidistant world map centered on the central United States shows how an amateur at that location would point a beam antenna for a short-path contact with a station in Cape Town, South Africa.

**G2D05** Which of the following is a good way to indicate on a clear frequency in the HF phone bands that you are looking for a contact with any station?

A. Sign your call sign once, followed by the words "listening for a call" — if no answer, change frequency and repeat

B. Say "QTC" followed by "this is" and your call sign — if no answer, change frequency and repeat

C. Repeat "CQ" a few times, followed by "this is," then your call sign a few times, then pause to listen, repeat as necessary

D. Transmit an unmodulated carried for approximately 10 seconds, followed by "this is" and your call sign, and pause to listen — repeat as necessary

**(C)** To call CQ on phone, you say "CQ CQ CQ, this is [your call repeated a few times using phonetics]". Then pause to listen for a station responding to your CQ. If no one answers, repeat your CQ as conditions require. [*General Class License Manual*, page 2-5]

**G2D06** How is a directional antenna pointed when making a "long-path" contact with another station?

A. Toward the rising sun

B. Along the grayline

C. 180 degrees from the station's short-path heading

D. Toward the north

**(C)** The shortest direct route, or great-circle path, between two points is called the short-path. If a directional antenna is pointed in exactly the opposite direction, 180 degrees different from the short-path, communications can be attempted on the long path. Long-path communication may be available when the more direct short path is closed. Because of the higher number of hops required, long path often works best when the path is across the ocean, a good reflector of HF signals. See **Figure G2.2**. [*General Class License Manual*, page 8-5]

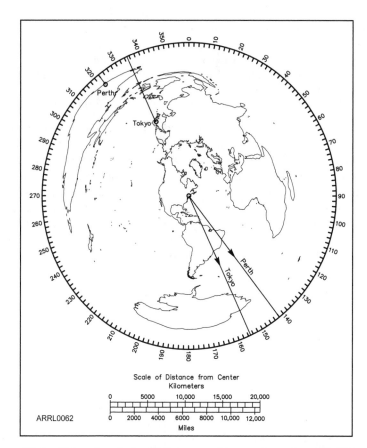

**Figure G2.2** —This azimuthal equidistant world map shows how W1AW in Newington, Connecticut would point a beam antenna to make a long-path contact with Tokyo, Japan or Perth, Australia. Notice that the both paths lie almost entirely over water, rather than land.

**G2D07**   Which of the following are examples of the NATO Phonetic Alphabet?

A.  Able, Baker, Charlie, Dog
B.  Adam, Boy, Charles, David
C.  America, Boston, Canada, Denmark
D.  Alpha, Bravo, Charlie, Delta

**(D)**   Phonetics are recommended for HF phone contacts just as they are on repeaters. The NATO phonetics (Alfa, Bravo, Charlie, Delta, and so on) are the most commonly used (see **www.arrl.org/files/file/Youth/Phonetic%20 Alphabet.pdf**. [*General Class License Manual*, page 2-2]

**G2D08    What is a reason why many amateurs keep a station log?**

A. The ITU requires a log of all international contacts
B. The ITU requires a log of all international third-party traffic
C. The log provides evidence of operation needed to renew a license without retest
D. To help with a reply if the FCC requests information

**(D)**    While useful, the FCC does not require you to keep a record (log) of your transmissions. It can be fun to keep a log, though, and then look back years later at the contacts you made. A log can also help document when your station was on the air and who was the control operator. You must give permission before a visiting amateur may operate your station. If you designate another amateur to be the control operator of your station, you both share the responsibility for the proper operation of the station. Unless your station records (log) show otherwise, the FCC will assume you were the control operator any time your station was operated. [*General Class License Manual*, page 2-6]

**G2D09    Which of the following is required when participating in a contest on HF frequencies?**

A. Submit a log to the contest sponsor
B. Send a QSL card to the stations worked, or QSL via Logbook of The World
C. Identify your station per normal FCC regulations
D. All these choices are correct

**(C)**    The fast-paced style of contest operating is quite popular on HF. The rules for identifying your station still apply during these competitive events. [*General Class License Manual*, page 2-5]

**G2D10    What is QRP operation?**

A. Remote piloted model control
B. Low-power transmit operation
C. Transmission using Quick Response Protocol
D. Traffic relay procedure net operation

**(B)**    QRP is a Q signal that means "lower your transmitter power." Many amateurs enjoy using low power levels for the challenge, the relative simplicity of the equipment, and sometimes to reduce interference. The generally accepted level for "QRP" power is 5 watts of transmitter output on CW and 10 W PEP output on phone. [*General Class License Manual*, page 3-14]

**G2D11** **Which of the following is typical of the lower HF frequencies during the summer?**

A. Poor propagation at any time of day
B. World-wide propagation during the daylight hours
C. Heavy distortion on signals due to photon absorption
D. High levels of atmospheric noise or "static"

**(D)** Atmospheric noise is most noticeable on the lower frequency HF bands in summer when storms are most common. [*General Class License Manual*, page 8-5]

## G2E — Digital operating procedures

**G2E01** **Which mode is normally used when sending RTTY signals via AFSK with an SSB transmitter?**

A. USB
B. DSB
C. CW
D. LSB

**(D)** Lower sideband (LSB) is used by convention for RTTY signals on all bands except 60 meters where USB must be used. There is no technical reason why LSB is preferred over USB for RTTY signals. [*General Class License Manual*, page 6-9]

**G2E02** **How can a PACTOR modem or controller be used to determine if the channel is in use by other PACTOR stations?**

A. Unplug the data connector temporarily and see if the channel-busy indication is turned off
B. Put the modem or controller in a mode which allows monitoring communications without a connection
C. Transmit UI packets several times and wait to see if there is a response from another PACTOR station
D. Send the message, "Is this frequency in use?"

**(B)** While full communications using PACTOR requires a connection between stations, it is possible to simply receive and display the data being exchanged without connecting. This is a common feature of digital communications called "monitor mode." You may not be able to understand the message or data being exchanged but you will be able to tell if communications using that particular mode is present. [*General Class License Manual*, page 6-7]

**G2E03** **What symptoms may result from other signals interfering with a PACTOR or WINMOR transmission?**

A. Frequent retries or timeouts
B. Long pauses in message transmission
C. Failure to establish a connection between stations
D. All these choices are correct

**(D)** Another signal of any mode that is present on the channel can interfere with a PACTOR or WINMOR transmission, causing errors in the received data. This results in a retransmission request (a "NAK" response). If the interference is strong enough, an error-free transmission may not be possible, causing the PACTOR or WINMOR stations to either fail to connect or exceed a limit for re-transmissions and terminate the connection. The interfering signal can also activate a "channel busy" detector which prevents a modem or protocol controller from transmitting until the interference stops. [*General Class License Manual*, page 6-14]

**G2E04** **What segment of the 20-meter band is most often used for digital transmissions (avoiding the DX propagation beacons)?**

A. 14.000 – 14.050 MHz
B. 14.070 – 14.112 MHz
C. 14.150 – 14.225 MHz
D. 14.275 – 14.350 MHz

**(B)** The FCC's rules specify where RTTY and data transmissions allowed, but the band plans tell you where such signals are usually found. The band plan in **Table G2.2** calls for RTTY and data operation from 14.070 to 14.112 MHz on 20 meters. [*General Class License Manual*, page 6-2]

---

**Table G2.2**
**ARRL Band Plan for RTTY/Data Frequencies**

| Band | RTTY/Data Frequencies | | |
| --- | --- | --- | --- |
| (Meters) | (MHz) | | |
| 160 | 1.800 | – | 1.810 |
| 80 | 3.570 | – | 3.600 |
| 40 | 7.080 | – | 7.125 |
| 30 | 10.130 | – | 10.140 |
| 20 | 14.070 | – | 14.0995 |
| | 14.1005 | – | 14.112 |
| 17 | 18.100 | – | 18.105 |
| 15 | 21.070 | – | 21.110 |
| 12 | 24.920 | – | 24.925 |
| 10 | 28.070 | – | 28.150 |

---

**G2E05** **What is the standard sideband used to generate a JT65, JT9, or FT8 digital signal when using AFSK in any amateur band?**

    A. LSB
    B. USB
    C. DSB
    D. SSB

**(B)** While RTTY uses LSB as the standard, JT65, JT9, and FT8 use USB. These modes are part of the WSJT suite of digital protocols used for meteor scatter, moonbounce (EME), and weak signal communications. [*General Class License Manual*, page 6-9]

**G2E06** **What is the most common frequency shift for RTTY emissions in the amateur HF bands?**

    A. 85 Hz
    B. 170 Hz
    C. 425 Hz
    D. 850 Hz

**(B)** The standard audio mark and space frequencies for encoding a RTTY signal are 2125 Hz (the mark tone) and 2295 Hz (the space tone). The difference between them is called the signal's shift. The rate of shifting between mark and space tones determines the character speed. On HF, the most common speed is 60 WPM (45 baud) with a 170 Hz shift. You should always answer a RTTY station at the same speed and shift it is using. [*General Class License Manual*, page 6-5]

**G2E07** **What segment of the 80-meter band is most commonly used for digital transmissions?**

    A. 3570 – 3600 kHz
    B. 3500 – 3525 kHz
    C. 3700 – 3750 kHz
    D. 3775 – 3825 kHz

**(A)** The FCC's rules specify where RTTY and data transmissions allowed, but the band plans tell you where such signals are usually found. The band plan calls for RTTY operation from 3570 to 3600 kHz on 80 meters. See the band plans in Table G2.2. [*General Class License Manual*, page 6-2]

**G2E08**   **In what segment of the 20-meter band are most PSK31 operations commonly found?**

A. At the bottom of the slow-scan TV segment, near 14.230 MHz
B. At the top of the SSB phone segment, near 14.325 MHz
C. In the middle of the CW segment, near 14.100 MHz
D. Below the RTTY segment, near 14.070 MHz

**(D)**    PSK signals are generally found in the vicinity of 14.070 MHz on the 20 meter band at the bottom of the RTTY/data area listed in Table G2.2. [*General Class License Manual*, page 6-2]


**G2E09**   **How do you join a contact between two stations using the PACTOR protocol?**

A. Send broadcast packets containing your call sign while in MONITOR mode
B. Transmit a steady carrier until the PACTOR protocol times out and disconnects
C. Joining an existing contact is not possible, PACTOR connections are limited to two stations
D. Send a NAK response continuously so that the sending station must stand by

**(C)**    The PACTOR and WINMOR protocols are designed to support communication between two stations so that errors can be corrected. The protocols do not support additional stations although you can monitor the communications as described in G2E02. [*General Class License Manual*, page 6-7]


**G2E10**   **Which of the following is a way to establish contact with a digital messaging system gateway station?**

A. Send an email to the system control operator
B. Send QRL in Morse code
C. Respond when the station broadcasts its SSID
D. Transmit a connect message on the station's published frequency

**(D)**    Message transfer is started by establishing a connection with the gateway station. This usually means transmitting a special "connect" message to that station on a published frequency. The gateway station usually operates without a control operator so it is up to you to make sure the channel is not being used by another station. [*General Class License Manual*, page 6-12]

**G2E11**   Which of the following is characteristic of the FT8 mode of the WSJT-X family?

A. It is a keyboard-to-keyboard chat mode
B. Each transmission takes exactly 60 seconds
C. It is limited to use on VHF
D. Typical exchanges are limited to call signs, grid locators, and signal reports

**(D)**   FT8 exchanges 75-bit messages (plus 12 bits for error detection codes) in a 50 Hz bandwidth. As FT8 is used today, there is a limited amount of information that can be exchanged, such as call signs, grid locators, and signal reports. [*General Class License Manual*, page 6-9]

**G2E12**   Which of the following connectors would be a good choice for a serial data port?

A. PL-259
B. Type N
C. Type SMA
D. DE-9

**(D)**   RS-232 serial data interfaces are common in amateur equipment, particularly older models. The most common connector used for these interfaces is the 9-pin D-style DE-9, also called a DB-9. RS-232 interfaces are rapidly being phased out in favor of serial interfaces that can transfer data at higher rates, such as USB and Bluetooth. [*General Class License Manual*, page 4-40]

**G2E13**   Which communication system sometimes uses the internet to transfer messages?

A. Winlink
B. RTTY
C. ARES
D. SKYWARN

**(A)**   The Winlink system is the best-known messaging system for Amateur Radio, accepting and delivering email messages via ham radio from a worldwide system of Internet servers. Other messaging systems such as APRS also use Internet gateway stations. [*General Class License Manual*, page 6-8]

**G2E14** **What could be wrong if you cannot decode an RTTY or other FSK signal even though it is apparently tuned in properly?**

A. The mark and space frequencies may be reversed
B. You may have selected the wrong baud rate
C. You may be listening on the wrong sideband
D. All these choices are correct

**(D)** There a number of software configuration choices that affect how RTTY signals are decoded and displayed. The symbol rate or baud must be correct as well as the MARK and SPACE tone frequencies. You might also have your receiver set to listen on the "wrong" sideband (LSB is the RTTY standard on the HF bands) or have a "reverse shift" option selected. It is often helpful when confronting this problem to have a friend help you get started by practicing sending and receiving. [*General Class License Manual*, page 6-9]

**G2E15** **Which of the following is a requirement when using the FT8 digital mode?**

A. A special hardware modem
B. Computer time accurate within approximately 1 second
C. Receiver attenuator set to –12 dB
D. A vertically polarized antenna

**(B)** Digital modes such as JT65 and FT8 also require transmissions to occur in precisely defined periods so the receiving systems know when to begin decoding. Utility software is available to keep your computer precisely synchronized to within 1 second of standard time. [*General Class License Manual*, page 6-6]

# Radio Wave Propagation

Your General class exam (Element 3) will consist of 35 questions taken from the General class question pool as prepared by the Volunteer Examiner Coordinators' Question Pool Committee. A certain number of questions are taken from each of the 10 subelements. There will be 3 questions from the subelement shown in this chapter. These questions are divided into 3 groups, labeled G3A through G3C.

## SUBELEMENT G3 — RADIO WAVE PROPAGATION
### [3 Exam Questions — 3 Groups]

## G3A — Sunspots and solar radiation; ionospheric disturbances; propagation forecasting and indices

**G3A01** What is the significance of the sunspot number with regard to HF propagation?

A. Higher sunspot numbers generally indicate a greater probability of good propagation at higher frequencies

B. Lower sunspot numbers generally indicate greater probability of sporadic E propagation

C. A zero sunspot number indicates that radio propagation is not possible on any band

D. A zero sunspot number indicates undisturbed conditions

**(A)**   A number of observatories around the world measure solar activity. A weighted average of this data is used to determine the International Sunspot Number (ISN) for each day. These daily sunspot counts are used to produce monthly and yearly average values. The average values are used to see trends and patterns in the measurements. See **Figure G3.1**. [*General Class License Manual*, page 8-7]

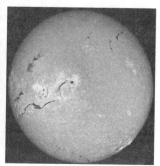

Figure G3.1 — Much more than sunspots can be seen when the sun is viewed through selective optical filters. This photo was taken through a hydrogen-alpha filter, which passes a narrow band of light wavelengths at 6562 angstroms (1 angstrom = $1 \times 10^{-10}$ meters). The bright patches are active areas around and often between sunspots. Dark irregular lines are filaments of activity having no central core. Faint magnetic field lines are visible around a large central sunspot group near the disc center. [Photo courtesy of Sacramento Peak Observatory, Sunspot, New Mexico]

**G3A02**    **What effect does a Sudden Ionospheric Disturbance have on the daytime ionospheric propagation of HF radio waves?**

A.  It enhances propagation on all HF frequencies
B.  It disrupts signals on lower frequencies more than those on higher frequencies
C.  It disrupts communications via satellite more than direct communications
D.  None, because only areas on the night side of the Earth are affected

**(B)**    A sudden ionospheric disturbance (SID) is often the result of solar flares that release large amounts of radiation. Ultraviolet and X-ray radiation from the sun travels at the speed of light, reaching the Earth in about eight minutes. When this radiation reaches the Earth, the level of ionization in the ionosphere increases rapidly. This causes D-layer absorption of radio waves to increase significantly. Absorption of radio signals in the D layer is always stronger at lower frequencies, affecting lower frequency signals more than higher frequency signals. [*General Class License Manual*, page 8-11]

**G3A03**    **Approximately how long does it take the increased ultraviolet and X-ray radiation from solar flares to affect radio propagation on Earth?**

A.  28 days
B.  1 to 2 hours
C.  8 minutes
D.  20 to 40 hours

**(C)**    Ultraviolet and X-ray radiation from the sun travels at the speed of light, reaching the Earth in about eight minutes (see **Figure G3.2**). [*General Class License Manual*, page 8-10]

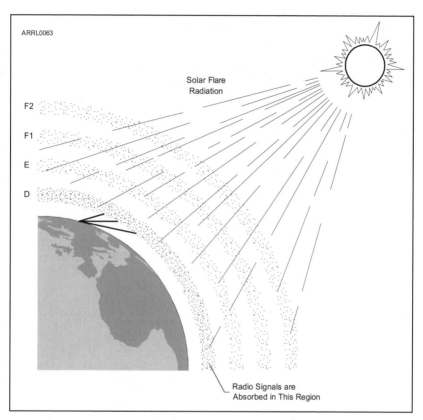

**Figure G3.2 — Approximately eight minutes after a solar flare occurs on the sun, the ultraviolet and X-ray radiation released by the flare reaches the Earth. This radiation causes increased ionization and radio-wave absorption in the D region of the ionosphere.**

**G3A04**  **Which of the following are least reliable for long-distance communications during periods of low solar activity?**

A.  80 meters and 160 meters
B.  60 meters and 40 meters
C.  30 meters and 20 meters
D.  15 meters, 12 meters, and 10 meters

**(D)**  The higher the frequency, the more ionization is needed in the ionosphere in order to refract (bend) the radio signal back to the Earth. When solar activity is low, signals at higher frequencies will pass through the ionosphere into space instead of being refracted back to Earth. During periods of low solar activity, the 15 meter (21 MHz), 12 meter (24.9 MHz) and 10 meter (28 MHz) bands are the least reliable HF bands for long distance communication. [*General Class License Manual*, page 8-7]

### G3A05   What is the solar flux index?

A. A measure of the highest frequency that is useful for ionospheric propagation between two points on Earth
B. A count of sunspots that is adjusted for solar emissions
C. Another name for the American sunspot number
D. A measure of solar radiation at 10.7 centimeters wavelength

**(D)**   Solar flux is the radio energy coming from the sun. High levels of solar energy produce greater ionization in the ionosphere. The solar flux measurement is taken daily by measuring radio energy from the sun at 2800 MHz which is a wavelength of 10.7 cm. The measurement is then converted into the solar flux index. Higher values of the solar flux index correspond to higher values of solar flux. The solar-flux measurement may be taken under any weather conditions — the sun does not have to be visible, as for determining the sunspot number. The radio energy measurement is converted to an open-ended numeric index with a minimum value of 65 (for the minimum amount of energy). Higher values of the solar flux index indicate higher levels of solar activity [*General Class License Manual*, page 8-9]

### G3A06   What is a geomagnetic storm?

A. A sudden drop in the solar flux index
B. A thunderstorm that affects radio propagation
C. Ripples in the ionosphere
D. A temporary disturbance in Earth's magnetosphere

**(D)**   Geomagnetic disturbances result when charged particles from a solar flare reach the Earth. When these charged particles reach the Earth's magnetic field, they are deflected toward the North and South poles. Radio communications along higher-latitude paths (latitudes greater than about 45 degrees) will be more affected than paths closer to the equator. The charged particles from the sun may make the F-region seem to disappear or seem to split into many layers, degrading or completely blacking out long-distance radio communications. [*General Class License Manual*, page 8-11]

### G3A07   At what point in the solar cycle does the 20-meter band usually support worldwide propagation during daylight hours?

A. At the summer solstice
B. Only at the maximum point of the solar cycle
C. Only at the minimum point of the solar cycle
D. At any point in the solar cycle

**(D)**   Even at the minimum point of the solar cycle, world-wide propagation is usually possible on the 20 meter band. As solar activity increases, the band will remain open for longer periods and with stronger signal strengths. For this reason, 20 meters is a favorite band for "DXers". [*General Class License Manual*, page 8-8]

**G3A08**   **Which of the following effects can a geomagnetic storm have on radio propagation?**

A. Improved high-latitude HF propagation
B. Degraded high-latitude HF propagation
C. Improved ground wave propagation
D. Degraded ground wave propagation

**(B)**     See G3A06. [*General Class License Manual*, page 8-12]


**G3A09**   **What benefit can high geomagnetic activity have on radio communications?**

A. Auroras that can reflect VHF signals
B. Higher signal strength for HF signals passing through the polar regions
C. Improved HF long path propagation
D. Reduced long delayed echoes

**(A)**     When sunspot numbers are high, there is a significant amount of solar activity and there will be more ionization of the ionosphere. The more the ionosphere is ionized, the higher the frequency of radio signals that may be used for long-distance communication. During the peak of a sunspot cycle, the 20 meter (14 MHz) band will be open around the world, even through the night. [*General Class License Manual*, page 8-12]


**G3A10**   **What causes HF propagation conditions to vary periodically in a roughly 28-day cycle?**

A. Long term oscillations in the upper atmosphere
B. Cyclic variation in Earth's radiation belts
C. The sun's rotation on its axis
D. The position of the moon in its orbit

**(C)**     It takes approximately 28 days for the sun to rotate on its axis. Since active areas on the sun may persist for more than one rotation, you can expect similar propagation conditions to recur approximately every 28 days. [*General Class License Manual*, page 8-8]


**G3A11**   **How long does it take charged particles from coronal mass ejections to affect radio propagation on Earth?**

A. 28 days
B. 14 days
C. 4 to 8 minutes
D. 20 to 40 hours

**(D)**     Plasma from the sun travels at speeds of two million miles per hour or more, so it can take about 20 to 40 hours for the plasma to travel the 93 million miles to Earth. [*General Class License Manual*, page 8-11]

### G3A12 What does the K-index indicate?

A. The relative position of sunspots on the surface of the sun
B. The short-term stability of Earth's magnetic field
C. The stability of the sun's magnetic field
D. The solar radio flux at Boulder, Colorado

**(B)** The K-index represents readings of the Earth's geomagnetic field, updated every three hours at Boulder, Colorado. K-index values indicate the stability of the Earth's geomagnetic field. Steady values indicate a stable geomagnetic field, while rising values indicate an active geomagnetic field. K-index trends are important indicators of changing propagation conditions. Rising K-index values are generally bad news for HF propagation, especially for propagation paths through latitudes above 30° north. Values of 4 and rising warn of conditions associated with auroras and degraded HF propagation. [*General Class License Manual*, page 8-9]

### G3A13 What does the A-index indicate?

A. The relative position of sunspots on the surface of the sun
B. The amount of polarization of the sun's electric field
C. The long-term stability of Earth's geomagnetic field
D. The solar radio flux at Boulder, Colorado

**(C)** The A-index is a daily figure for the state of activity of the Earth's magnetic field. The A-index tells you mainly about yesterday's conditions, but it is very revealing when charted regularly, because geomagnetic disturbances nearly always recur at four-week intervals. (It takes the sun 28 days to rotate once on its axis.) [*General Class License Manual*, page 8-9]

### G3A14 How are radio communications usually affected by the charged particles that reach Earth from solar coronal holes?

A. HF communications are improved
B. HF communications are disturbed
C. VHF/UHF ducting is improved
D. VHF/UHF ducting is disturbed

**(B)** The corona is the sun's outer layer. Temperatures in the corona are typically about two million degrees Celsius, but can be more than four million degrees Celsius above an active sunspot region. A coronal hole is an area of somewhat lower temperature. Matter ejected through such a "hole" is in the form of plasma, a highly ionized gas made up of electrons, protons and neutral particles. If the "jet" of material is directed toward the Earth it can result in a geomagnetic storm on Earth, disrupting HF communications. [*General Class License Manual*, page 8-12]

## G3B — Maximum Usable Frequency; Lowest Usable Frequency; propagation

**G3B01**     **What is a characteristic of skywave signals arriving at your location by both short-path and long-path propagation?**

A. Periodic fading approximately every 10 seconds
B. Signal strength increased by 3 dB
C. The signal might be cancelled causing severe attenuation
D. A slightly delayed echo might be heard

**(D)**     Normally, you will expect radio signals to arrive at your station by following the shortest possible path between you and the transmitting station. This is called short-path propagation. Signals that might have arrived from the opposite direction, 180 degrees different from the short-path signals are normally so weak that you would probably not hear them. Signals that arrive 180 degrees from the short path are called long-path signals. When propagation conditions are suitable, the long-path signals may be strong enough to support communication. In fact, there are times when the long-path propagation may be even better than the short-path propagation. Stations with directional antennas can point their antennas directly away from each other to communicate. (This is not simply communicating using signal radiated "off the back" of the antennas.) If you are listening to signals on your receiver and you hear a well-defined echo, even if it is a weak echo, the chances are you are hearing signals arrive at your station over the long path. The slightly longer time it takes the signals to travel the longer distance around the Earth results in a slight delay when compared to the direct, short-path signals. This is a good indication that you may be able to point your antenna directly away from the received station to communicate. [*General Class License Manual*, page 8-6]

### G3B02    What factors affect the MUF?

A. Path distance and location
B. Time of day and season
C. Solar radiation and ionospheric disturbances
D. All these choices are correct

**(D)**    Maximum Usable Frequency (MUF) is the highest frequency that will provide skywave propagation between two specific locations. For example, suppose you live in Illinois and want to communicate with another amateur in Ecuador. You might find that the MUF for this contact is about 18 MHz at 1400 UTC. You may also find that the MUF to communicate with a station in Spain at that same time is 12 MHz. Different distances and directions will often result in very different MUF values. The MUF depends on conditions in the ionosphere, and those conditions will vary by time of day as well as the season of the year. The amount of solar radiation striking the ionosphere (see **Figure G3.3**) varies significantly depending on the timing of the 11-year sunspot cycle. Any solar flares, coronal-mass ejections and other disturbances on the sun can also result in ionospheric disturbances that will affect the MUF. Answer choices A, B and C all describe factors that will affect the MUF for a given skywave propagation path, so answer choice D is correct. [*General Class License Manual*, page 8-9]

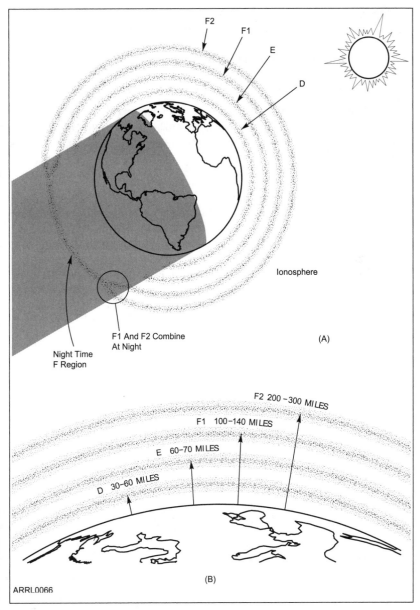

**Figure G3.3 — The ionosphere consists of several regions of ionized particles at different heights above the Earth. At night, the D and E regions disappear and the F1 and F2 regions combine to form a single F region.**

### G3B03 Which of the following applies when selecting a frequency for lowest attenuation when transmitting on HF?

A. Select a frequency just below the MUF
B. Select a frequency just above the LUF
C. Select a frequency just below the critical frequency
D. Select a frequency just above the critical frequency

**(A)**  Ionospheric absorption (attenuation) is lowest just below the Maximum Usable Frequency (MUF). Use a frequency just below the MUF for the highest received signal strength. (See also G3B05.) [*General Class License Manual*, page 8-10]

### G3B04 What is a reliable way to determine if the MUF is high enough to support skip propagation between your station and a distant location on frequencies between 14 and 30 MHz?

A. Listen for signals from an international beacon in the frequency range you plan to use
B. Send a series of dots on the band and listen for echoes from your signal
C. Check the strength of TV signals from western Europe
D. Check the strength of signals in the MF AM broadcast band

**(A)**  Beacon stations transmit signals so that amateur operators can evaluate propagation conditions. For example, by listening for beacon stations from Western Europe, you will be able to determine if the MUF is high enough for 10 meter communications to that area. (See also G3B05.) [*General Class License Manual*, page 8-10]

### G3B05 What usually happens to radio waves with frequencies below the MUF and above the LUF when they are sent into the ionosphere?

A. They are bent back to Earth
B. They pass through the ionosphere
C. They are amplified by interaction with the ionosphere
D. They are bent and trapped in the ionosphere to circle Earth

**(A)**  The Maximum Usable Frequency (MUF) relates to a particular desired destination. The MUF is the highest frequency that will allow the radio wave to reach its desired destination using E or F-region propagation. There is no single MUF for a given transmitter location; it will vary depending on the direction and distance to the station you are attempting to contact. Signals at frequencies lower than the MUF are generally bent back to Earth, while those higher than the MUF will pass through the ionosphere instead of being bent back to the Earth. See **Figure G3.4**. [*General Class License Manual*, page 8-10]

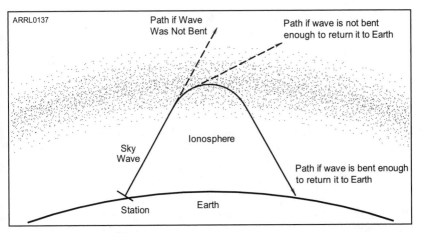

**Figure G3.4 — Radio waves are bent in the ionosphere, so they return to Earth far from the transmitter. If the radio wave is not bent (refracted) enough in the ionosphere, it will pass into space rather than returning to Earth.**

**G3B06** **What usually happens to radio waves with frequencies below the LUF?**

A. They are bent back to Earth
B. They pass through the ionosphere
C. They are completely absorbed by the ionosphere
D. They are bent and trapped in the ionosphere to circle Earth

**(C)** The Lowest Usable Frequency (LUF) is the frequency below which ionospheric absorption attenuates the radio signals to below the atmospheric noise levels. Since absorption increases with decreasing frequency, signals at frequencies below the LUF cannot be received via skywave communication. [*General Class License Manual*, page 8-10]

**G3B07** **What does LUF stand for?**

A. The Lowest Usable Frequency for communications between two points
B. The Longest Universal Function for communications between two points
C. The Lowest Usable Frequency during a 24-hour period
D. The Longest Universal Function during a 24-hour period

**(A)** See G3B06. [*General Class License Manual*, page 8-9]

**G3B08    What does MUF stand for?**

A. The Minimum Usable Frequency for communications between two points
B. The Maximum Usable Frequency for communications between two points
C. The Minimum Usable Frequency during a 24-hour period
D. The Maximum Usable Frequency during a 24-hour period

**(B)**    The Maximum Usable Frequency (MUF) relates to a particular desired destination. The MUF is the highest frequency that will allow the radio wave to reach its desired destination using skywave propagation. There is no single MUF for a given transmitter location; it will vary depending on the direction and distance to the station you are attempting to contact. Signals at frequencies lower than the MUF are generally bent back to Earth, while signals with frequencies higher than the MUF will pass through the ionosphere instead of being bent back to the Earth. [*General Class License Manual*, page 8-9]


**G3B09    What is the approximate maximum distance along the Earth's surface that is normally covered in one hop using the F2 region?**

A. 180 miles
B. 1,200 miles
C. 2,500 miles
D. 12,000 miles

**(C)**    Layers in the F region form and decay in correlation with the daily passage of the sun. The F1 and F2 layers form when the F region splits into two parts due to high radiation from the sun, recombining into a single F layer at night. The more solar radiation the F region receives, the more it is ionized so it reaches maximum ionization shortly after noon during the summertime. The ionization tapers off very gradually towards sunset and the F2 layer remains usable into the night. The F2 region is the highest of the ionosphere, reaching as high as 300 miles at noon in the summertime. Because it is the highest, it is the region mainly responsible for long-distance communications. A one-hop transmission can travel a maximum distance of about 2,500 miles using F2 propagation. See **Figure G3.5**. [*General Class License Manual*, page 8-2]

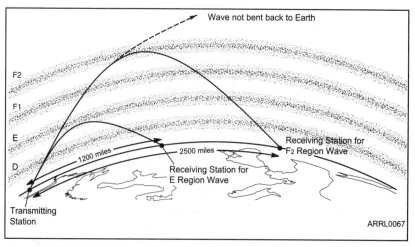

Figure G3.5 — Radio waves are refracted (bent) in the ionosphere and may return to Earth. If the radio waves are refracted to Earth from the F2 region, they may return to Earth about 2500 miles from the transmitting station. If the radio waves are refracted to Earth from the E region, they may return to Earth about 1200 miles from the transmitting station

**G3B10** What is the approximate maximum distance along the Earth's surface that is normally covered in one hop using the E region?

A. 180 miles
B. 1,200 miles
C. 2,500 miles
D. 12,000 miles

**(B)** The E region of the ionosphere is the second lowest, just above the D region. The E layer forms at an altitude of about 70 miles above the Earth. The E region ionizes during the daytime, but does not stay ionized very long after sunset. Ionization in the E region is at a maximum around midday. During the daytime, a radio signal can travel a maximum distance of about 1,200 miles in one hop using E-region propagation. [*General Class License Manual*, page 8-2]

**G3B11** **What happens to HF propagation when the LUF exceeds the MUF?**

A. No HF radio frequency will support ordinary skywave communications over the path
B. HF communications over the path are enhanced
C. Double hop propagation along the path is more common
D. Propagation over the path on all HF frequencies is enhanced

**(A)** Signals at frequencies below the LUF will be absorbed in the ionosphere rather than returning to Earth. Occasionally the LUF may be higher than the maximum usable frequency (MUF). This means that for the highest possible signal frequency that will propagate through the ionosphere for that path, the absorption is so large that even signals at the MUF are absorbed. Under these conditions it is impossible to establish skywave communication between those two points no matter what frequency is used! (Communications between either of the two locations and other locations may be possible, since the LUF and MUF depend on the end points of the communication path.) [*General Class License Manual*, page 8-10]

## G3C — Ionospheric layers; critical angle and frequency; HF scatter; Near Vertical Incidence Skywave

**G3C01** **Which ionospheric layer is closest to the surface of Earth?**

A. The D layer
B. The E layer
C. The F1 layer
D. The F2 layer

**(A)** The D region of the ionosphere is the lowest, forming the D layer at a height of 30 to 60 miles. Because it is the lowest, it is also the densest and its ionization disappears by dark. [*General Class License Manual*, page 8-2]

**G3C02** **Where on Earth do ionospheric layers reach their maximum height?**

A. Where the sun is overhead
B. Where the sun is on the opposite side of Earth
C. Where the sun is rising
D. Where the sun has just set

**(A)** The F region forms and decays in correlation with the daily passage of the sun. The F1 and F2 layers form when the F region splits into two parts due to receiving high radiation from the sun, recombining into a single F region at night. The more solar radiation the F region receives, the more it is ionized so it reaches maximum ionization shortly after noon during the summertime. The ionization tapers off very gradually toward sunset and the F2 region remains usable into the night. The F2 region is the highest of the ionosphere, reaching as high as 300 miles at noon in the summertime. [*General Class License Manual*, page 8-2]

**G3C03**   **Why is the F2 region mainly responsible for the longest distance radio wave propagation?**

A. Because it is the densest ionospheric layer
B. Because of the Doppler effect
C. Because it is the highest ionospheric region
D. Because of meteor trails at that level

**(C)**      Because the F2 region is the highest ionospheric region, it is the region mainly responsible for long-distance communications. A signal can travel a maximum distance of about 2500 miles via one-hop from the F2 region. [*General Class License Manual*, page 8-2]

**G3C04**   **What does the term "critical angle" mean, as used in radio wave propagation?**

A. The long path azimuth of a distant station
B. The short path azimuth of a distant station
C. The lowest takeoff angle that will return a radio wave to Earth under specific ionospheric conditions
D. The highest takeoff angle that will return a radio wave to Earth under specific ionospheric conditions

**(D)**      At each frequency there is a maximum angle for which the radio wave can leave the antenna and still be refracted back to Earth by the ionosphere instead of simply passing through it and proceeding out into space. The critical angle changes depending on the ionization of the ionosphere. See **Figure G3.6**. [*General Class License Manual*, page 8-2]

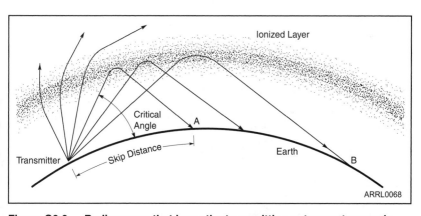

**Figure G3.6 — Radio waves that leave the transmitting antenna at an angle higher than the critical angle are not refracted enough to return to Earth. A radio wave at the critical angle will return to Earth. The lowest-angle wave will return to Earth farther away than the wave at the critical angle. This illustrates the importance of low radiation angles for working DX.**

**G3C05**   **Why is long-distance communication on the 40-meter, 60-meter, 80-meter, and 160-meter bands more difficult during the day?**

A. The F layer absorbs signals at these frequencies during daylight hours
B. The F layer is unstable during daylight hours
C. The D layer absorbs signals at these frequencies during daylight hours
D. The E layer is unstable during daylight hours

**(C)**   Think of the D region as the Darned Daylight region. Instead of bending high frequency signals back to Earth, it absorbs energy from them. Signals at lower frequencies (longer wavelengths such as 160, 80, 60 and 40 meters) are absorbed more than at higher frequencies. The ionization created by the sunlight does not last very long in the D region, disappearing at or shortly after sunset. See **Figure G3.7**. [*General Class License Manual*, page 8-5]

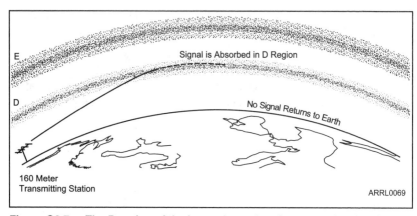

**Figure G3.7 — The D region of the ionosphere absorbs energy from radio waves. Lower-frequency radio waves don't make it all the way through the D region, so the waves do not return to Earth. Higher-frequency waves travel through the D region, and are then refracted (bent) back to Earth.**

### G3C06    What is a characteristic of HF scatter?

- A. Phone signals have high intelligibility
- B. Signals have a fluttering sound
- C. There are very large, sudden swings in signal strength
- D. Scatter propagation occurs only at night

**(B)**      The area between the farthest reach of ground-wave propagation and the point where signals are refracted back from the ionosphere (skywave propagation) is called the skip zone. Since some of the transmitted signal is scattered in the atmosphere or from ground reflections, communication may be possible in the skip zone by the use of scatter signals. The amount of signal scattered in the atmosphere will be quite small and the signal received in the skip zone will arrive from several paths. This tends to produce a weak, distorted signal with a fluttering or wavering sound. See **Figure G3.8**. [*General Class License Manual*, page 8-12]

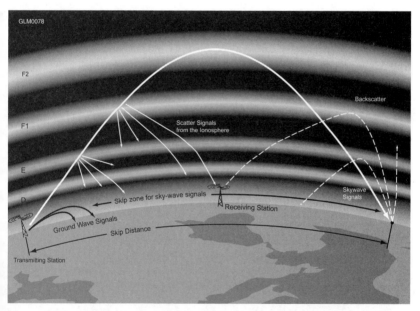

**Figure G3.8 — Radio waves may be reflected back towards the transmitting station from variations in the ionosphere or after striking the ground after ionospheric reflection. Some of this energy may be scattered back into the skip zone as a weak, highly variable signal.**

**G3C07** **What makes HF scatter signals often sound distorted?**

A. The ionospheric layer involved is unstable
B. Ground waves are absorbing much of the signal
C. The E-region is not present
D. Energy is scattered into the skip zone through several different radio wave paths

**(D)** The amount of signal scattered back toward the transmitting station from the ionosphere or ground will be quite small. The signal received in the skip zone will also arrive from several radio-wave paths. This tends to produce a weak, distorted signal with a fluttering or wavering sound. (See also G3C06.) [*General Class License Manual*, page 8-12]

**G3C08** **Why are HF scatter signals in the skip zone usually weak?**

A. Only a small part of the signal energy is scattered into the skip zone
B. Signals are scattered from the magnetosphere, which is not a good reflector
C. Propagation is through ground waves, which absorb most of the signal energy
D. Propagation is through ducts in the F region, which absorb most of the energy

**(A)** See G3C07. [*General Class License Manual*, page 8-12]

**G3C09** **What type of propagation allows signals to be heard in the transmitting station's skip zone?**

A. Faraday rotation
B. Scatter
C. Chordal hop
D. Short-path

**(B)** The area between the farthest reach of ground-wave propagation and the point where signals are refracted back from the ionosphere (skywave propagation) is called the skip zone. Since some of the transmitted signal is scattered in the atmosphere, communication may be possible in the skip zone by the use of scatter signals. (See also G3C06.) [*General Class License Manual*, page 8-12]

### G3C10 What is Near Vertical Incidence Skywave (NVIS) propagation?

A. Propagation near the MUF
B. Short distance MF or HF propagation using high elevation angles
C. Long path HF propagation at sunrise and sunset
D. Double hop propagation near the LUF

**(B)** Near Vertical Incidence Skywave (NVIS) propagation refers to communication using skywave signals transmitted at very high vertical angles. The frequencies used are below the critical frequency, meaning that their critical angle (see question G3C04) is ninety degrees, meaning they can be reflected straight back down to Earth. Because the signals travel at high angles, they have a minimum amount of attenuation from the D and E layers. The result is good communications in a region around the transmitter over distances higher than supported by ground-wave propagation. See **Figure G3.9**. [*General Class License Manual*, page 8-12]

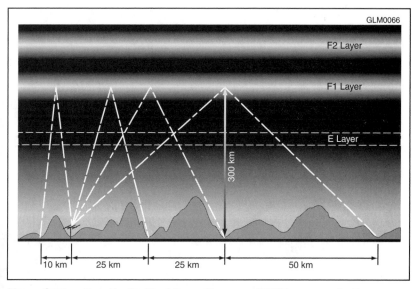

Figure G3.9 — Near Vertical Incidence Sky-wave (NVIS) communications relies on signals below the critical frequency transmitted at high vertical angles. The signals are reflected by the ionosphere back to Earth in the region around the transmitter.

**G3C11**    **Which ionospheric layer is the most absorbent of long skip signals during daylight hours on frequencies below 10 MHz?**

A. The F2 layer
B. The F1 layer
C. The E layer
D. The D layer

**(D)**    See G3C05. [*General Class License Manual*, page 8-5]

# Amateur Radio Practices

Your General class exam (Element 3) will consist of 35 questions taken from the General class question pool as prepared by the Volunteer Examiner Coordinators' Question Pool Committee. A certain number of questions are taken from each of the 10 subelements. There will be 5 questions from the subelement shown in this chapter. These questions are divided into 5 groups, labeled G4A through G4E.

## SUBELEMENT G4 — AMATEUR RADIO PRACTICES
### [5 Exam Questions — 5 groups]

### G4A — Station operation and setup

**G4A01** What is the purpose of the notch filter found on many HF transceivers?

A. To restrict the transmitter voice bandwidth
B. To reduce interference from carriers in the receiver passband
C. To eliminate receiver interference from impulse noise sources
D. To enhance the reception of a specific frequency on a crowded band

**(B)** A notch filter removes a very narrow band of frequencies — the "notch" — from its input. This allows the notch filter to get rid of an interfering tone, such as from an unmodulated carrier, while maintaining the intelligibility of the desired signal. An automatic notch filter can detect the presence of steady tones and remove them without operator intervention. [*General Class License Manual*, page 5-20]

**G4A02** What is one advantage of selecting the opposite, or "reverse," sideband when receiving CW signals on a typical HF transceiver?

A. Interference from impulse noise will be eliminated
B. More stations can be accommodated within a given signal passband
C. It may be possible to reduce or eliminate interference from other signals
D. Accidental out-of-band operation can be prevented

**(C)** Interference from nearby signals can often be avoided by switching the receiver's carrier frequency to the opposite side of the desired signal, without changing its audio pitch. This won't work on SSB because it also inverts the spectrum of the speech, rendering it unintelligible. [*General Class License Manual*, page 5-20]

**G4A03** **What is normally meant by operating a transceiver in "split" mode?**

A. The radio is operating at half power
B. The transceiver is operating from an external power source
C. The transceiver is set to different transmit and receive frequencies
D. The transmitter is emitting an SSB signal, as opposed to DSB operation

**(C)** Operating split means using one VFO for transmitting and another for receiving. This is often used when a rare DX station is on the air with many callers. Operating simplex — transmitting and receiving on the same frequency — can result in a lot of confusion with stations trying to hear the DX station while others transmit. By transmitting on one frequency and having callers transmit somewhere else (usually on adjacent frequencies) everyone can hear the DX station and keep "in sync" for more orderly, effective operating. [*General Class License Manual*, page 2-4]

**G4A04** **What reading on the plate current meter of a vacuum tube RF power amplifier indicates correct adjustment of the plate tuning control?**

A. A pronounced peak
B. A pronounced dip
C. No change will be observed
D. A slow, rhythmic oscillation

**(B)** See G4A08. [*General Class License Manual*, page 5-15]

**G4A05** **What is a reason to use Automatic Level Control (ALC) with an RF power amplifier?**

A. To balance the transmitter audio frequency response
B. To reduce harmonic radiation
C. To reduce distortion due to excessive drive
D. To increase overall efficiency

**(C)** The ALC circuit of an RF power amplifier senses the amount of input power and generates a feedback voltage to keep the transmitter from generating too much power for the amplifier input. This helps prevent spurious emissions that cause interference to other stations. Note that ALC should not be used with digital signals since it can result in distortion of the signal's waveform. (See also G4A14.) [*General Class License Manual*, page 5-15]

**G4A06**   **What type of device is often used to match transmitter output impedance to an impedance not equal to 50 ohms?**

A. Balanced modulator
B. SWR bridge
C. Antenna coupler or antenna tuner
D. Q multiplier

**(C)**    There are many names for devices that use LC circuits to convert one impedance to another — antenna coupler, impedance matching unit, transmatch, and antenna tuner are common. [*General Class License Manual*, page 7-22]

**G4A07**   **What condition can lead to permanent damage to a solid-state RF power amplifier?**

A. Insufficient drive power
B. Low input SWR
C. Shorting the input signal to ground
D. Excessive drive power

**(D)**    Transistors are more sensitive to input drive levels than more rugged vacuum tubes and can be damaged very quickly if too much power is applied. Fast-acting control circuits are required to protect the transistors from excessive input drive power. [*General Class License Manual*, page 5-15]

**G4A08**   **What is the correct adjustment for the load or coupling control of a vacuum tube RF power amplifier?**

A. Minimum SWR on the antenna
B. Minimum plate current without exceeding maximum allowable grid current
C. Highest plate voltage while minimizing grid current
D. Maximum power output without exceeding maximum allowable plate current

**(D)**    The TUNE control of a vacuum tube RF amplifier sets the impedance matching circuit to resonance at the frequency of operation. With transmitter power applied, the TUNE control is adjusted until a pronounced dip in plate current indicates that the circuit is resonant at the operating frequency. The LOAD or COUPLING control is then used to adjust the amount of output power. The TUNE and LOAD controls are alternately adjusted until the required amount of output power is obtained without exceeding the tube's plate current rating. [*General Class License Manual*, page 5-15]

### G4A09 Why is a time delay sometimes included in a transmitter keying circuit?

A. To prevent stations from interfering with one another
B. To allow the transmitter power regulators to charge properly
C. To allow time for transmit-receive changeover operations to complete properly before RF output is allowed
D. To allow time for a warning signal to be sent to other stations

**(C)** If a relay switches while RF is present in the circuit that is called hot switching. At high power levels hot switching can damage the relay, so it is important to let the relay complete switching before energizing the circuit. Similarly, it is important to disconnect sensitive receive circuits before transmitter RF is enabled. A controlled time delay, called sequencing is used to ensure that all relay and switching operations are completed before enabling the transmitter. [*General Class License Manual*, page 5-14]

### G4A10 What is the purpose of an electronic keyer?

A. Automatic transmit/receive switching
B. Automatic generation of strings of dots and dashes for CW operation
C. VOX operation
D. Computer interface for PSK and RTTY operation

**(B)** Electronic keyers eliminate a lot of the manual work involved in operating a straight key and ensure that each dot or dash has the right length and spacing. This allows comfortable high-speed Morse operation even for extended periods of time. [*General Class License Manual*, page 2-13]

### G4A11 Which of the following is a use for the IF shift control on a receiver?

A. To avoid interference from stations very close to the receive frequency
B. To change frequency rapidly
C. To permit listening on a different frequency from that on which you are transmitting
D. To tune in stations that are slightly off frequency without changing your transmit frequency

**(A)** Passband or IF shift adjusts the receiver's passband above or below the displayed carrier frequency to avoid interfering signals. This results in a shift in tone of the received signal, but often improves intelligibility. [*General Class License Manual*, page 5-20]

**G4A12** **Which of the following is a common use for the dual-VFO feature on a transceiver?**

A. To allow transmitting on two frequencies at once
B. To permit full duplex operation — that is, transmitting and receiving at the same time
C. To permit monitoring of two different frequencies
D. To facilitate computer interface

**(C)** Dual VFOs are used for split operation where it can be very useful to listen to the DX station's transmit and receive frequencies. Another use for dual VFOs is to monitor one frequency continuously while operating on another frequency. (See also G4A03.) [*General Class License Manual*, page 2-4]

**G4A13** **What is one reason to use the attenuator function that is present on many HF transceivers?**

A. To reduce signal overload due to strong incoming signals
B. To reduce the transmitter power when driving a linear amplifier
C. To reduce power consumption when operating from batteries
D. To slow down received CW signals for better copy

**(A)** Too strong an input signal can overload a receiver, creating distortion products that interfere with reception of the desired signal. Using an attenuator reduces the input signal level and potential receiver overload. [*General Class License Manual*, page 5-19]

**G4A14** **What is likely to happen if a transceiver's ALC system is not set properly when transmitting AFSK signals with the radio using single sideband mode?**

A. ALC will invert the modulation of the AFSK mode
B. Improper action of ALC distorts the signal and can cause spurious emissions
C. When using digital modes, too much ALC activity can cause the transmitter to overheat
D. All these choices are correct

**(B)** For operation on digital modes, it is important that the output waveform be undistorted. By setting the transmitter output power so that the ALC circuit does not activate, that ensures the output amplifier is operating with maximum linearity. [*General Class License Manual*, page 6-11]

**G4A15** **Which of the following can be a symptom of transmitted RF being picked up by an audio cable carrying AFSK data signals between a computer and a transceiver?**

A. The VOX circuit does not un-key the transmitter
B. The transmitter signal is distorted
C. Frequent connection timeouts
D. All these choices are correct

**(D)** RF signals picked up by cables connected to the microphone input can cause audio input circuits to operate improperly. This can cause distortion of the audio signal which makes the digital signal hard to decode. Because it causes the audio input circuits to act as if an audio signal is present, RF can also cause the VOX circuit to stay activated even if the audio signal is no longer present. [*General Class License Manual*, page 5-22]

**G4A16** **How does a noise blanker work?**

A. By temporarily increasing received bandwidth
B. By redirecting noise pulses into a filter capacitor
C. By reducing receiver gain during a noise pulse
D. By clipping noise peaks

**(C)** Most receivers also provide noise blankers and noise reduction features. Noise blankers operate by sensing short, sharp pulses in the IF signals and quickly reduce the gain of IF and audio amplifiers during the pulse. This is called blanking. [*General Class License Manual*, page 5-20]

**G4A17** **What happens as the noise reduction control level in a receiver is increased?**

A. Received signals may become distorted
B. Received frequency may become unstable
C. CW signals may become severely attenuated
D. Received frequency may shift several kHz

**(A)** Noise reduction is performed on the receiver's output audio by DSP. This system attempts to remove hiss and noise from the audio that is not part of the desired speech, data, or CW. There may be more than one noise reduction setting optimized for different types of signals. Increasing the noise reduction level may cause some of the desired signal to be removed as well, causing distortion. Use the least noise reduction required to minimize distortion. [*General Class License Manual*, page 5-20]

## G4B — Test and monitoring equipment; two-tone test

**G4B01**   What item of test equipment contains horizontal and vertical channel amplifiers?

A. An ohmmeter
B. A signal generator
C. An ammeter
D. An oscilloscope

**(D)**   An analog oscilloscope uses one signal to deflect a beam of electrons horizontally across the face of the screen and a second signal to deflect them vertically. The electron beam causes a phosphor coating on the inside of the screen to glow so that the beam's position, representing the input signal voltages, can be observed. Digital oscilloscopes convert the signals to data and display it on a computer-like screen to show voltages in the same way. Some oscilloscopes also accept a second input signal which allows two signals to be compared to each other at the same time. [*General Class License Manual*, page 4-42]

**G4B02**   Which of the following is an advantage of an oscilloscope versus a digital voltmeter?

A. An oscilloscope uses less power
B. Complex impedances can be easily measured
C. Input impedance is much lower
D. Complex waveforms can be measured

**(D)**   Digital voltmeters display measured values of voltage with excellent precision but they cannot measure a complex signal waveform's time-related behavior, such as frequency, or how it reacts to other signals. [*General Class License Manual*, page 4-42]

**G4B03**   Which of the following is the best instrument to use when | checking the keying waveform of a CW transmitter?

A. An oscilloscope
B. A field strength meter
C. A sidetone monitor
D. A wavemeter

**(A)**   An oscilloscope visually displays a signal waveform. This allows you to observe the shape of the CW signal's rise and fall time of the signal and the shape of signal's envelope. It also allows you to observe problems such as flat-topping (caused by overmodulation) on your SSB signal. [*General Class License Manual*, page 4-42]

**G4B04** **What signal source is connected to the vertical input of an oscilloscope when checking the RF envelope pattern of a transmitted signal?**

A. The local oscillator of the transmitter
B. An external RF oscillator
C. The transmitter balanced mixer output
D. The attenuated RF output of the transmitter

**(D)** When the RF output from a transmitter is connected to the vertical channel of an oscilloscope, the oscilloscope visually displays the signal's envelope. This allows you to check for signal distortion such as flat-topping (caused by overmodulation). Use an attenuator or RF sampling device to limit the voltage at the oscilloscope input. [*General Class License Manual*, page 4-42]

**G4B05** **Why is high input impedance desirable for a voltmeter?**

A. It improves the frequency response
B. It decreases battery consumption in the meter
C. It improves the resolution of the readings
D. It decreases the loading on circuits being measured

**(D)** The higher the impedance of a voltmeter, the smaller the amount of current drawn from the circuit being tested. This allows the voltmeter to make an accurate measurement of voltage while disturbing the circuit as little as possible. [*General Class License Manual*, page 4-41]

**G4B06** **What is an advantage of a digital voltmeter as compared to an analog voltmeter?**

A. Better for measuring computer circuits
B. Better for RF measurements
C. Better precision for most uses
D. Faster response

**(C)** A digital voltmeter displays measurements of voltage, current and resistance in numeric form instead of using a moving needle and a fixed scale. That results in significantly better precision than an analog meter. Analog meters, however, may be a better choice for adjusting a circuit for maximum and minimum values because the needle movement is easier to see than it is to evaluate changes of a numeric display. [*General Class License Manual*, page 4-41]

**G4B07** **What signals are used to conduct a two-tone test?**

A. Two audio signals of the same frequency shifted 90 degrees
B. Two non-harmonically related audio signals
C. Two swept frequency tones
D. Two audio frequency range square wave signals of equal amplitude

**(B)** See G4B15. [*General Class License Manual*, page 5-11]

**G4B08** **Which of the following instruments may be used to monitor relative RF output when making antenna and transmitter adjustments?**

A. A field strength meter
B. An antenna noise bridge
C. A multimeter
D. A Q meter

**(A)** A field strength meter makes a relative measurement of the intensity of the field being radiated from an antenna. Some amateurs keep a field strength meter in their shack to monitor the relative RF output from their station. This can be especially handy when you are making antenna or transmitter adjustments. [*General Class License Manual*, page 4-43]

**G4B09** **Which of the following can be determined with a field strength meter?**

A. The radiation resistance of an antenna
B. The radiation pattern of an antenna
C. The presence and amount of phase distortion of a transmitter
D. The presence and amount of amplitude distortion of a transmitter

**(B)** By placing a field-strength meter in different locations around the antenna, you can determine the relative field pattern of the antenna. (See also G4B08.) [*General Class License Manual*, page 4-43]

**G4B10** **Which of the following can be determined with a directional wattmeter?**

A. Standing wave ratio
B. Antenna front-to-back ratio
C. RF interference
D. Radio wave propagation

**(A)** SWR can be calculated from forward and reflected power measurements made using a directional wattmeter. SWR is then calculated using the following formula:

$$SWR = \frac{1+\sqrt{P_R / P_F}}{1-\sqrt{P_R / P_F}}$$

where $P_F$ is forward power and $P_R$ is reflected power. [*General Class License Manual*, page 4-43]

**G4B11** Which of the following must be connected to an antenna analyzer when it is being used for SWR measurements?

A. Receiver
B. Transmitter
C. Antenna and feed line
D. All these choices are correct

**(C)** An antenna analyzer is the equivalent of a very low power, adjustable-frequency transmitter and SWR bridge. The antenna and feed line are connected to the analyzer and SWR measurements are made directly from the analyzer's meter or display while the analyzer frequency is adjusted. This is much more convenient than using a transmitter and wattmeter and also minimizes the potential for interfering with other signals. [*General Class License Manual*, page 4-42]

**G4B12** What problem can occur when making measurements on an antenna system with an antenna analyzer?

A. Permanent damage to the analyzer may occur if it is operated into a high SWR
B. Strong signals from nearby transmitters can affect the accuracy of measurements
C. The analyzer can be damaged if measurements outside the ham bands are attempted
D. Connecting the analyzer to an antenna can cause it to absorb harmonics

**(B)** Because an analyzer's SWR bridge must be sensitive enough to work with the low-power transmitter, it is also sensitive to RF that the antenna may pick up. This is a particular problem when using the analyzer near broadcast stations with their high-powered transmitters. Symptoms might include SWR readings that change with station programming and excessively high or low SWR that does not change with frequency as expected. [*General Class License Manual*, page 4-43]

**G4B13** What is a use for an antenna analyzer other than measuring the SWR of an antenna system?

A. Measuring the front-to-back ratio of an antenna
B. Measuring the turns ratio of a power transformer
C. Determining the impedance of coaxial cable
D. Determining the gain of a directional antenna

**(C)** An antenna analyzer's manual will show how to make many useful measurements such as feed line characteristic impedance, velocity of propagation, electrical length, and so on. These are very flexible test instruments. [*General Class License Manual*, page 4-43]

**G4B14** **What is an instance in which the use of an instrument with analog readout may be preferred over an instrument with digital readout?**
A. When testing logic circuits
B. When high precision is desired
C. When measuring the frequency of an oscillator
D. When adjusting tuned circuits

**(D)** The analog meter's moving needle across calibrated scales on the meter face is much easier to adjust for a maximum or minimum value than a numeric display. [*General Class License Manual*, page 4-41]

**G4B15** **What type of transmitter performance does a two-tone test analyze?**
A. Linearity
B. Percentage of suppression of carrier and undesired sideband for SSB
C. Percentage of frequency modulation
D. Percentage of carrier phase shift

**(A)** It is common to test the amplitude linearity of a single-sideband transmitter by injecting two audio tones of equal level into the microphone input, then observing the pattern made on an oscilloscope. In order to get meaningful results, the two tones must not be harmonically related to each other (such as 1 and 2 kHz). Of course, in order for the audio frequencies to display on the oscilloscope, they must be within the audio passband of the transmitter. The ARRL Lab uses 700 Hz and 1900 Hz tones to perform this test. [*General Class License Manual*, page 5-11]

## G4C — Interference to consumer electronics; grounding; DSP

**G4C01** **Which of the following might be useful in reducing RF interference to audio frequency devices?**
A. Bypass inductor
B. Bypass capacitor
C. Forward-biased diode
D. Reverse-biased diode

**(B)** If radio frequency interference is entering a home audio system through external control cables or power leads, a bypass capacitor can be effective at keeping the unwanted RF signal out of the equipment. With transistor or integrated circuit audio amplifiers you may need to use RF chokes in series with the speaker leads instead of a bypass capacitor. See the *ARRL Handbook* and *The ARRL RFI Book* for more information on finding and fixing RFI problems. [*General Class License Manual*, page 5-24]

**G4C02**  **Which of the following could be a cause of interference covering a wide range of frequencies?**

A. Not using a balun or line isolator to feed balanced antennas
B. Lack of rectification of the transmitter's signal in power conductors
C. Arcing at a poor electrical connection
D. Using a balun to feed an unbalanced antenna

**(C)**  An arc, such as in motors or at the contacts of electrical equipment, is rich in harmonic energy, even though the primary current may be dc or 60 Hz ac. The resulting RF harmonics can be radiated by the power wiring as broadband noise heard by nearby receivers. Broadband noise can also be caused by intermittent or poor contacts in RF circuits in your own station. [*General Class License Manual*, page 5-24]

**G4C03**  **What sound is heard from an audio device or telephone if there is interference from a nearby single sideband phone transmitter?**

A. A steady hum whenever the transmitter is on the air
B. On-and-off humming or clicking
C. Distorted speech
D. Clearly audible speech

**(C)**  An audio device or telephone can sometimes rectify and detect RF signals in much the same way that an AM broadcast radio does. The audio signal is then amplified resulting in interference. The amateur's voice will be heard but it will be highly distorted. [*General Class License Manual*, page 5-24]

**G4C04**  **What is the effect on an audio device when there is interference from a nearby CW transmitter?**

A. On-and-off humming or clicking
B. A CW signal at a nearly pure audio frequency
C. A chirpy CW signal
D. Severely distorted audio

**(A)**  See G4C03 — the amateur's CW transmission will be heard as on-and-off humming or clicking in a Morse code-like pattern. [*General Class License Manual*, page 5-24]

**G4C05** **What might be the problem if you receive an RF burn when touching your equipment while transmitting on an HF band, assuming the equipment is connected to a ground rod?**

A. Flat braid rather than round wire has been used for the ground wire
B. Insulated wire has been used for the ground wire
C. The ground rod is resonant
D. The ground wire has high impedance on that frequency

**(D)** If the connection to a ground rod is long enough, it can be an odd multiple of ¼-wavelength long on one or more bands. This resonance results in the wire having a high impedance on that band, which enables high RF voltages to be present on the chassis of your equipment or microphone. The high voltage will cause an RF burn if the "hot spot" is touched when you are transmitting. RF burns are painful but rarely cause significant injury. The ARRL's Safety web page (**www.arrl.org/safety**) includes a great deal of useful information about station grounding and managing RF voltage and current [*General Class License Manual*, page 5-23]

**G4C06** **What effect can be caused by a resonant ground connection?**

A. Overheating of ground straps
B. Corrosion of the ground rod
C. High RF voltages on the enclosures of station equipment
D. A ground loop

**(C)** See G4C05. [*General Class License Manual*, page 5-23]

**G4C07** **Why should soldered joints not be used with the wires that connect the base of a tower to a system of ground rods?**

A. The resistance of solder is too high
B. Solder flux will prevent a low conductivity connection
C. Solder has too high a dielectric constant to provide adequate lightning protection
D. A soldered joint will likely be destroyed by the heat of a lightning strike

**(D)** Do not use solder to make the connections since solder joints would likely melt and be destroyed if hit with a lightning-sized current pulse. Use mechanical clamps, brazing, or welding to be sure the ground connection is heavy enough. [*General Class License Manual*, page 9-8]

**G4C08** Which of the following would reduce RF interference caused by common-mode current on an audio cable?

A. Placing a ferrite choke around the cable
B. Adding series capacitors to the conductors
C. Adding shunt inductors to the conductors
D. Adding an additional insulating jacket to the cable

**(A)** The best solution to many types of interference caused by proximity to an amateur station is to keep the RF signals from entering the equipment in the first place. If filters can be used, they are generally the most effective and least troublesome to install. The next approach is to prevent RF current from flowing by placing inductance or resistance in its path. This is done by forming the conductor carrying the RF current into an RF choke, winding it around or through a ferrite core. Ferrite beads and cores can also be placed on cables to prevent RF common-mode current from flowing on the outside of cable braids or shields. [*General Class License Manual*, page 5-24]

**G4C09** How can a ground loop be avoided?

A. Connect all ground conductors in series
B. Connect the AC neutral conductor to the ground wire
C. Avoid using lock washers and star washers when making ground connections
D. Connect all ground conductors to a single point

**(D)** Ground loops are created when a continuous current path (the loop) exists through a series of equipment enclosures and cables. The loop acts as a single-turn inductor that picks up voltages from magnetic fields generated by power transformers, ac wiring and other low-frequency currents. The result is a hum or buzz in audio signals or an ac signal that interferes with control or data signals. Less frequently, the loop can pick up transmitted RF and cause distortion in audio signals. Since the many interconnections in an amateur station make it impossible to avoid loops, minimize the loop's area and inductance by using short cables and bundling them together. [*General Class License Manual*, page 5-23]

**G4C10** What could be a symptom of a ground loop somewhere in your station?

A. You receive reports of "hum" on your station's transmitted signal
B. The SWR reading for one or more antennas is suddenly very high
C. An item of station equipment starts to draw excessive amounts of current
D. You receive reports of harmonic interference from your station

**(A)** See G4C09. [*General Class License Manual*, page 5-23]

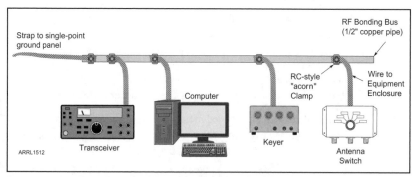

**Figure G4.1 — A typical bonding bus for a station with equipment on a table or desk. By connecting equipment together using short, heavy connections, voltage differences are minimized.**

**G4C11**   **What technique helps to minimize RF "hot spots" in an amateur station?**

A. Building all equipment in a metal enclosure
B. Using surge suppressor power outlets
C. Bonding all equipment enclosures together
D. Low-pass filters on all feed lines

**(C)**   The basics for RF bonding in your station are:

• Connect all metal equipment enclosures directly together or to a common RF bonding bus (see **Figure G4.1**).

• Keep all connections, straps and wires short.

• Use short, heavy conductors such as heavy wire (#12 or #14 AWG) or strap.

Where strong RF signals are present, a piece of wide flashing or screen can be placed under the equipment and connected to the RF bonding bus. [*General Class License Manual*, page 5-22]

**G4C12**   **Which of the following is an advantage of a receiver DSP IF filter as compared to an analog filter?**

A. A wide range of filter bandwidths and shapes can be created
B. Fewer digital components are required
C. Mixing products are greatly reduced
D. The DSP filter is much more effective at VHF frequencies

**(A)**   Because DSP uses software to process the digitized signal, the number of different functions which can be performed is only limited by the amount of memory and processing speed. In addition, unlike most analog filters, parameters such as bandwidth and the shape of the response can be made adjustable by the operator. This provides a great deal of flexibility in receiver operation. [*General Class License Manual*, page 5-18]

### G4C13  Why must the metal enclosure of every item of station equipment be grounded?

A. It prevents a blown fuse in the event of an internal short circuit
B. It prevents signal overload
C. It ensures that the neutral wire is grounded
D. It ensures that hazardous voltages cannot appear on the chassis

**(D)**　Any equipment with an exposed metal enclosure must be grounded. This prevents hazardous voltages from appearing on the equipment chassis, creating a shock hazard. [*General Class License Manual*, page 5-22]

## G4D — Speech processors; S meters; sideband operation near band edges

### G4D01  What is the purpose of a speech processor as used in a modern transceiver?

A. Increase the intelligibility of transmitted phone signals during poor conditions
B. Increase transmitter bass response for more natural-sounding SSB signals
C. Prevent distortion of voice signals
D. Decrease high-frequency voice output to prevent out-of-band operation

**(A)**　A speech processor can improve signal intelligibility by raising average power without increasing peak envelope power (PEP). It does this by amplifying low-level signals more than high-level signals. As a result, the average signal level is increased. A speech processor does not increase the transmitter output PEP. See **Figure G4.2**. [*General Class License Manual*, page 5-12]

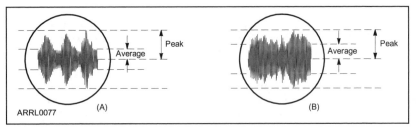

**Figure G4.2 — A typical SSB voice-modulated signal might have an envelope similar to the oscilloscope display shown at A. After speech processing, the envelope pattern might look like the display at B. The average power of the processed signal has increased, but the PEP is unchanged.**

**G4D02** **Which of the following describes how a speech processor affects a transmitted single sideband phone signal?**

A. It increases peak power
B. It increases average power
C. It reduces harmonic distortion
D. It reduces intermodulation distortion

**(B)** See G4D01. [*General Class License Manual*, page 5-12]


**G4D03** **Which of the following can be the result of an incorrectly adjusted speech processor?**

A. Distorted speech
B. Splatter
C. Excessive background pickup
D. All these choices are correct

**(D)** Proper adjustment of a speech processor is important to ensure your transmitted signal is not distorted and is free of spurious signals. Excessive processing causes your speech to be distorted. Processors can also amplify background noise from fans and other radios and combine them with your desired speech. Another common result of too much processing is overdriving the transmitter output stages, causing interference ("splatter") to signals on nearby frequencies. Read the owner's manual for your radio and learn to operate its speech processor. Practice on the air with a friend to insure you are adjusting the processor correctly. [*General Class License Manual*, page 5-12]

**G4D04** **What does an S meter measure?**

A. Conductance
B. Impedance
C. Received signal strength
D. Transmitter power output

**(C)** An S-meter measures received signal strength in S-units. [*General Class License Manual*, page 5-19]

**G4D05** **How does a signal that reads 20 dB over S9 compare to one that reads S9 on a receiver, assuming a properly calibrated S meter?**

A. It is 10 times less powerful
B. It is 20 times less powerful
C. It is 20 times more powerful
D. It is 100 times more powerful

**(D)** An ideal S-meter operates on a logarithmic scale, indicating one S-unit of change for a four-times increase or decrease in power. (This is a 6-dB change in power.) Most actual S-meters are only calibrated to that standard in the middle of their range (if at all). Above S-9, theoretically corresponding to a 50 µV input signal, S-meters are calibrated in dB. In the example of this question, a signal 20 dB stronger than S-9 is 100 times stronger than S-9. [*General Class License Manual*, page 5-19]

**G4D06** **Where is an S meter found?**

A. In a receiver
B. In an SWR bridge
C. In a transmitter
D. In a conductance bridge

**(A)** An S-meter measures received signal strength in a receiver or the receive circuits of a transceiver. [*General Class License Manual*, page 5-19]

**G4D07** **How much must the power output of a transmitter be raised to change the S meter reading on a distant receiver from S8 to S9?**

A. Approximately 1.5 times
B. Approximately 2 times
C. Approximately 4 times
D. Approximately 8 times

**(C)** For an ideal S-meter, one S-unit of change corresponds to a four-times increase or decrease in power. This is a 6 dB change in power. (See also G4D05.) [*General Class License Manual*, page 5-19]

**G4D08** **What frequency range is occupied by a 3 kHz LSB signal when the displayed carrier frequency is set to 7.178 MHz?**

A. 7.178 to 7.181 MHz
B. 7.178 to 7.184 MHz
C. 7.175 to 7.178 MHz
D. 7.1765 to 7.1795 MHz

**(C)** Nearly all radios display the carrier frequency of a SSB transmission. That means your actual signal lies entirely above (USB) or below (LSB) the displayed frequency. If the sidebands occupy 3 kHz of spectrum, you'll need to stay far enough from the edge of your frequency privileges to avoid transmitting a signal outside them. For example, Generals are permitted to use up to 14.350 MHz, so the displayed carrier frequency of a 3 kHz-wide USB signal should be no less than 3 kHz from the band edge — 14.347 MHz — and the signal occupies 14.347 to 14.350 MHz. If you transmit higher than that, the sidebands begin to extend into the non-amateur frequencies above 14.350 MHz! Similarly, using 3 kHz-wide LSB on 40 meters, Generals should operate with the carrier frequency no less than 3 kHz above the band edge — 7.178 MHz — thus occupying the range of 7.175 to 7.178 MHz. See **Figure G4.3**. [*General Class License Manual*, page 5-12]

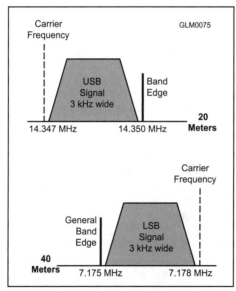

Figure G4.3 — When the sidebands of a typical 3 kHz-wide SSB signal extend from the carrier towards a band edge or a band segment edge, operate with a displayed carrier frequency no closer than 3 kHz to the edge frequency and be sure your signal is "clean."

**G4D09** What frequency range is occupied by a 3 kHz USB signal with the displayed carrier frequency set to 14.347 MHz?

A. 14.347 to 14.647 MHz
B. 14.347 to 14.350 MHz
C. 14.344 to 14.347 MHz
D. 14.3455 to 14.3485 MHz

**(B)**    See G4D08. [*General Class License Manual*, page 5-12]


**G4D10** How close to the lower edge of the phone segment should your displayed carrier frequency be when using 3 kHz wide LSB?

A. At least 3 kHz above the edge of the segment
B. At least 3 kHz below the edge of the segment
C. At least 1 kHz below the edge of the segment
D. At least 1 kHz above the edge of the segment

**(A)**    See G4D08. [*General Class License Manual*, page 5-12]


**G4D11** How close to the upper edge of the phone segment should your displayed carrier frequency be when using 3 kHz wide USB?

A. At least 3 kHz above the edge of the band
B. At least 3 kHz below the edge of the band
C. At least 1 kHz above the edge of the segment
D. At least 1 kHz below the edge of the segment

**(B)**    See G4D08. [*General Class License Manual*, page 5-12]


## G4E — HF mobile radio installations; alternative energy source operation

**G4E01** What is the purpose of a capacitance hat on a mobile antenna?

A. To increase the power handling capacity of a whip antenna
B. To allow automatic band changing
C. To electrically lengthen a physically short antenna
D. To allow remote tuning

**(C)**    A structure of rods and possibly a ring added at or near the top of the antenna is called a capacitance hat or capacity hat. It increases the capacitance of a mobile antenna and electrically lengthens it so that it can be used effectively at lower frequencies. [*General Class License Manual*, page 7-6]

### G4E02 What is the purpose of a corona ball on an HF mobile antenna?

A. To narrow the operating bandwidth of the antenna
B. To increase the "Q" of the antenna
C. To reduce the chance of damage if the antenna should strike an object
D. To reduce RF voltage discharge from the tip of the antenna while transmitting

**(D)** The sharp tip of mobile whip can result in corona discharge from high RF voltages even at moderate power levels. By adding a smooth ball, the tendency for corona to form is reduced [*General Class License Manual*, page 7-6]

### G4E03 Which of the following direct, fused power connections would be the best for a 100 watt HF mobile installation?

A. To the battery using heavy-gauge wire
B. To the alternator or generator using heavy-gauge wire
C. To the battery using resistor wire
D. To the alternator or generator using resistor wire

**(A)** When you are making the power connections for your 100-watt HF radio for mobile operation, connect heavy-gauge wires directly to the battery terminals. Both leads should have fuses, placed as close to the battery as possible. See **Figure G4.4**. [*General Class License Manual*, page 5-21]

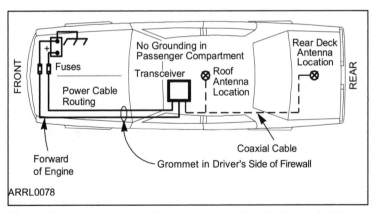

**Figure G4.4 — A typical mobile transceiver's installation and wiring system.**

**G4E04**  **Why is it best NOT to draw the DC power for a 100 watt HF transceiver from a vehicle's auxiliary power socket?**

A. The socket is not wired with an RF-shielded power cable
B. The socket's wiring may be inadequate for the current drawn by the transceiver
C. The DC polarity of the socket is reversed from the polarity of modern HF transceivers
D. Drawing more than 50 watts from this socket could cause the engine to overheat

**(B)** The auxiliary socket wiring is adequate for a low-power hand-held radio but not for a full-power HF transceiver drawing 20 amps or more when transmitting. Use a direct connection to the battery. (See also G4E03.) [*General Class License Manual*, page 5-21]


**G4E05**  **Which of the following most limits an HF mobile installation?**

A. "Picket fencing"
B. The wire gauge of the DC power line to the transceiver
C. Efficiency of the electrically short antenna
D. FCC rules limiting mobile output power on the 75-meter band

**(C)** HF mobile antenna systems are the most limiting factor for effective operation of your station. Placing even an 8-foot vertical antenna on top of a small car makes a dangerously tall system. If you have a taller vehicle, this kind of antenna is almost out of the question. Some type of inductive loading to shorten the length is then required. For operation on the 75 meter band this compromise results in a relatively inefficient antenna system. [*General Class License Manual*, page 5-21]


**G4E06**  **What is one disadvantage of using a shortened mobile antenna as opposed to a full size antenna?**

A. Short antennas are more likely to cause distortion of transmitted signals
B. Short antennas can only receive circularly polarized signals
C. Operating bandwidth may be very limited
D. Harmonic radiation may increase

**(C)** Electrically short antennas present a very low impedance at their base, the usual location of the feed point. This causes the frequency range to be very narrow over which a matching network presents a 50 ohm impedance to the transmitter. [*General Class License Manual*, page 7-6]

**G4E07** **Which of the following may cause receive interference in an HF radio installed in a vehicle?**

A. The battery charging system
B. The fuel delivery system
C. The vehicle control computer
D. All these choices are correct

**(D)** High-current pulses and switching from the battery charging system can easily create signals at RF which can cause interference. Similarly, the dc motors associated with electric fuel pumps are also frequent sources of interference. Digital signals internal and external to the vehicle's control computer system can radiate from the vehicle's electrical wiring and be received at RF, as well. [*General Class License Manual*, page 5-22]

**G4E08** **What is the name of the process by which sunlight is changed directly into electricity?**

A. Photovoltaic conversion
B. Photon emission
C. Photosynthesis
D. Photon decomposition

**(A)** Photovoltaic conversion by solar cells and panels converts sunlight directly into dc current. Natural sources of energy are becoming more economical and more practical as a way to power your station. [*General Class License Manual*, page 4-36]

**G4E09** **What is the approximate open-circuit voltage from a fully illuminated silicon photovoltaic cell?**

A. 0.02 VDC
B. 0.5 VDC
C. 0.2 VDC
D. 1.38 VDC

**(B)** Each photovoltaic cell produces about 0.5 volt in full sunlight if there is no load connected to the cell. The size or surface area of the cell determines the maximum current that the cell can supply. [*General Class License Manual*, page 4-36]

**G4E10** **What is the reason that a series diode is connected between a solar panel and a storage battery that is being charged by the panel?**

A. The diode serves to regulate the charging voltage to prevent overcharge

B. The diode prevents self-discharge of the battery through the panel during times of low or no illumination

C. The diode limits the current flowing from the panel to a safe value

D. The diode greatly increases the efficiency during times of high illumination

**(B)** If connected directly to a battery, during periods of low or no illumination, the battery voltage will be higher than that from the panel, allowing the battery to discharge back through the panel. [*General Class License Manual*, page 4-39]

**G4E11** **Which of the following is a disadvantage of using wind as the primary source of power for an emergency station?**

A. The conversion efficiency from mechanical energy to electrical energy is less than 2 percent

B. The voltage and current ratings of such systems are not compatible with amateur equipment

C. A large energy storage system is needed to supply power when the wind is not blowing

D. All these choices are correct

**(C)** Wind systems need to have a storage battery to supply electricity when the wind is not blowing. [*General Class License Manual*, page 4-39]

# Electrical Principles

Your General class exam (Element 3) will consist of 35 questions taken from the General class question pool as prepared by the Volunteer Examiner Coordinators' Question Pool Committee. A certain number of questions are taken from each of the 10 subelements. There will be 3 questions from the subelement shown in this chapter. These questions are divided into 3 groups, labeled G5A through G5C.

## SUBELEMENT G5 — ELECTRICAL PRINCIPLES
### [3 Exam Questions — 3 Groups]

### G5A — Reactance; inductance; capacitance; impedance; impedance matching

**G5A01**    What is impedance?
- A. The electric charge stored by a capacitor
- B. The inverse of resistance
- C. The opposition to the flow of current in an AC circuit
- D. The force of repulsion between two similar electric fields

**(C)**    Impedance is the opposition to the flow of current in an alternating current (ac) circuit caused by capacitive reactance, inductive reactance, and resistance. [*General Class License Manual*, page 4-21]

**G5A02**    What is reactance?
- A. Opposition to the flow of direct current caused by resistance
- B. Opposition to the flow of alternating current caused by capacitance or inductance
- C. A property of ideal resistors in AC circuits
- D. A large spark produced at switch contacts when an inductor is de-energized

**(B)**    The opposition to flow of ac current caused by inductance and capacitance is referred to as reactance. Reactance is one component of impedance, along with resistance. [*General Class License Manual*, page 4-19]

### G5A03 Which of the following causes opposition to the flow of alternating current in an inductor?

A. Conductance
B. Reluctance
C. Admittance
D. Reactance

**(D)** The opposition to flow of current in an alternating current (ac) circuit caused by an inductor is referred to as inductive reactance. (See also G5A02.) [*General Class License Manual*, page 4-19]

### G5A04 Which of the following causes opposition to the flow of alternating current in a capacitor?

A. Conductance
B. Reluctance
C. Reactance
D. Admittance

**(C)** The opposition to flow of current in an alternating current (ac) circuit caused by a capacitor is referred to as capacitive reactance. (See also G5A02.) [*General Class License Manual*, page 4-19]

### G5A05 How does an inductor react to AC?

A. As the frequency of the applied AC increases, the reactance decreases
B. As the amplitude of the applied AC increases, the reactance increases
C. As the amplitude of the applied AC increases, the reactance decreases
D. As the frequency of the applied AC increases, the reactance increases

**(D)** Inductive reactance increases as the ac frequency increases. (See also G5A03.) [*General Class License Manual*, page 4-20]

### G5A06 How does a capacitor react to AC?

A. As the frequency of the applied AC increases, the reactance decreases
B. As the frequency of the applied AC increases, the reactance increases
C. As the amplitude of the applied AC increases, the reactance increases
D. As the amplitude of the applied AC increases, the reactance decreases

**(A)** Capacitive reactance decreases as the ac frequency increases. (See also G5A04.) [*General Class License Manual*, page 4-19]

**G5A07** **What happens when the impedance of an electrical load is equal to the output impedance of a power source, assuming both impedances are resistive?**

A. The source delivers minimum power to the load
B. The electrical load is shorted
C. No current can flow through the circuit
D. The source can deliver maximum power to the load

**(D)** A power source delivers maximum power to a load when the impedance of the load is equal to (matched to) the impedance of the source. (This is only true for ac power when both impedances are entirely resistive and have no reactance.) When the impedances are not matched, the power source cannot transfer as much power to the load. [*General Class License Manual*, page 4-22]

**G5A08** **What is one reason to use an impedance matching transformer?**

A. To minimize transmitter power output
B. To maximize the transfer of power
C. To reduce power supply ripple
D. To minimize radiation resistance

**(B)** An impedance matching transformer changes the ratio of voltage and current between the load and source. Since impedance is the ratio of voltage and current, the transformer can also match different impedances. Matching impedances also maximizes power transfer between the source and load. [*General Class License Manual*, page 4-22]

**G5A09** **What unit is used to measure reactance?**

A. Farad
B. Ohm
C. Ampere
D. Siemens

**(B)** The ohm is the unit used to measure any opposition to the flow of current. In an ac circuit, this opposition is referred to as impedance which includes both reactance and resistance. [*General Class License Manual*, page 4-19]

**G5A10** **Which of the following devices can be used for impedance matching at radio frequencies?**

A. A transformer
B. A Pi-network
C. A length of transmission line
D. All these choices are correct

**(D)** All of these can alter the ratio of voltage and current in a circuit, changing the impedance as well. (See G5A08 and G5A11.) Special lengths of transmission lines can be used to set up patterns of reflections in the feed line that cancel the reflections from a mismatched load, making the load impedance appear as if it was the same as that of the feed line. [*General Class License Manual*, page 4-22]

**G5A11** **Which of the following describes one method of impedance matching between two AC circuits?**

A. Insert an LC network between the two circuits
B. Reduce the power output of the first circuit
C. Increase the power output of the first circuit
D. Insert a circulator between the two circuits

**(A)** An LC network, such as a pi-network (see G5A10), uses the exchange of stored energy between the inductor and capacitors to transform the ratio of voltage and current (impedance) at its input and output while transferring power between them. Common examples of impedance matching LC networks are the L-, T-, and Pi-network, named for the resemblance to a letter of the arrangement of their components on a schematic. [*General Class License Manual*, page 4-22]

## G5B — The decibel; current and voltage dividers; electrical power calculations; sine wave root-mean-square (RMS) values; PEP calculations

**G5B01** What dB change represents a factor of two increase or decrease in power?

A. Approximately 2 dB
B. Approximately 3 dB
C. Approximately 6 dB
D. Approximately 12 dB

**(B)** The decibel scale is a logarithmic scale in which a two-times increase (or decrease) in power is represented by 3 dB. The mathematical formula for the decibel scale for power is:

$$dB = 10 \times \log_{10}\left(\frac{P_2}{P_1}\right)$$

where $P_1$ = reference power and $P_2$ = power being compared to the reference value.

In this case:

$$dB = 10 \times \log_{10}\left(\frac{2}{1}\right) = 10 \times \log_{10}(2) = 10 \times 0.3 = 3\,dB$$

[*General Class License Manual*, page 4-2]

---

### Table G5.1

### Some Common Decibel Values and Power Ratio Equivalents

| dB | $P_2 / P_1$ |
|---|---|
| 20 | 100 ($10^2$) |
| 10 | 10 ($10^1$) |
| 6 | 4 |
| 3 | 2 |
| 0 | 1 |
| −3 | 0.5 |
| −6 | 0.25 |
| −10 | 0.1 ($10^{-1}$) |
| −20 | 0.01 ($10^{-2}$) |

---

**G5B02** **How does the total current relate to the individual currents in each branch of a purely resistive parallel circuit?**

A. It equals the average of each branch current
B. It decreases as more parallel branches are added to the circuit
C. It equals the sum of the currents through each branch
D. It is the sum of the reciprocal of each individual voltage drop

**(C)** In a circuit with several parallel branches, the total current flowing into the junction of the branches is equal to the sum of the current through each branch. This is Kirchoff's Current Law. See **Figure G5.1**. [*General Class License Manual*, page 4-15]

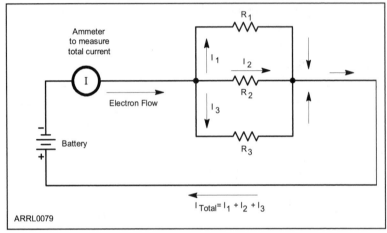

**Figure G5.1 — The sum of the current flowing into a junction point (node) in a circuit must be equal to the current flowing out of the junction point (node). This principle is called Kirchhoff's Current Law, named for Gustav Kirchhoff, the German scientist who discovered it.**

**G5B03**   How many watts of electrical power are used if 400 VDC is supplied to an 800 ohm load?

    A.  0.5 watts
    B.  200 watts
    C.  400 watts
    D.  3200 watts

**(B)**   Since P = I × E and I = E/R, the power in a circuit also can be expressed as

$$P = \frac{E \times E}{R}$$

In this case:

$$P = \frac{400 \times 400}{800} = \frac{160,000}{800} = 200 \text{ W}$$

[*General Class License Manual*, page 4-1]

**G5B04**   How many watts of electrical power are used by a 12 VDC light bulb that draws 0.2 amperes?

    A.  2.4 watts
    B.  24 watts
    C.  6 watts
    D.  60 watts

**(A)**   Use the Power Circle (**Figure G5.2**) to find the equation for calculating power. In this case, power is equal to the voltage times the current: P = I × E = 0.2 × 12 = 2.4 watts. [*General Class License Manual*, page 4-2]

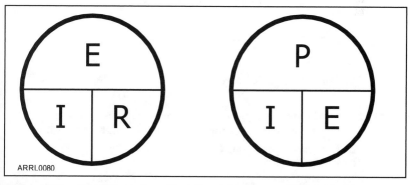

**Figure G5.2 — The "Ohm's Law Circle" and the "Power Circle" will help you remember the equations that include voltage, current, resistance and power. Cover the letter representing the unknown quantity to find an equation to calculate that quantity. If you cover the I in the Ohm's Law Circle, you are left with E/R. If you cover the P in the Power Circle, you are left with I × E. Combining these terms, you can write the equation to calculate power when you know the voltage and the resistance.**

**G5B05** How many watts are dissipated when a current of 7.0 milliamperes flows through a 1250 ohm resistance?

A. Approximately 61 milliwatts
B. Approximately 61 watts
C. Approximately 11 milliwatts
D. Approximately 11 watts

**(A)** Use the Ohm's Law Circle and Power Circle drawings to find the equations to calculate power. Since P = I × E and E = R × I, the power in a circuit can also be expressed as P = I × I × R, so P = 0.007 × 0.007 × 1250 = 0.06125 W = 61.25 mW. Remember that 7 milliamperes is equal to 0.007 ampere, 1.25 kilohms is equal to 1250 ohms and 0.06125 watt is equal to approximately 61 milliwatts. [*General Class License Manual*, page 4-2]

**G5B06** What is the output PEP from a transmitter if an oscilloscope measures 200 volts peak-to-peak across a 50 ohm dummy load connected to the transmitter output?

A. 1.4 watts
B. 100 watts
C. 353.5 watts
D. 400 watts

**(B)** PEP is the output power of one complete RF cycle at the peak of the signal's envelope and is equal to:

$$PEP = \frac{(\text{Peak envelope voltage} \times 0.707)^2}{R}$$

Peak envelope voltage = Peak-to-peak envelope voltage / 2, so:

$$PEP = \frac{(100 \times 0.707)^2}{50} = 100 \text{ W}$$

[*General Class License Manual*, page 4-6]

**G5B07** What value of an AC signal produces the same power dissipation in a resistor as a DC voltage of the same value?

A. The peak-to-peak value
B. The peak value
C. The RMS value
D. The reciprocal of the RMS value

**(C)** RMS, or root mean square, voltage values convert a constantly-varying ac voltage to the equivalent of a constant dc voltage. The RMS value of an ac voltage would deliver the same amount of power to a resistance as a dc voltage of the same value. [*General Class License Manual*, page 4-5]

**G5B08** What is the peak-to-peak voltage of a sine wave with an RMS voltage of 120.0 volts?

A. 84.8 volts
B. 169.7 volts
C. 240.0 volts
D. 339.4 volts

**(D)** $V_{PK-PK} = V_{RMS} \times 1.414 \times 2 = 120 \times 1.414 \times 2 = 339.4$ V [*General Class License Manual*, page 4-5]

**G5B09** What is the RMS voltage of a sine wave with a value of 17 volts peak?

A. 8.5 volts
B. 12 volts
C. 24 volts
D. 34 volts

**(B)** If you know the peak voltage, you can find the RMS value by multiplying the peak voltage by 0.707 (which is the same as dividing by the square root of 2): $17 \times 0.707 = 12$ V. See **Figure G5.3**. [*General Class License Manual*, page 4-5]

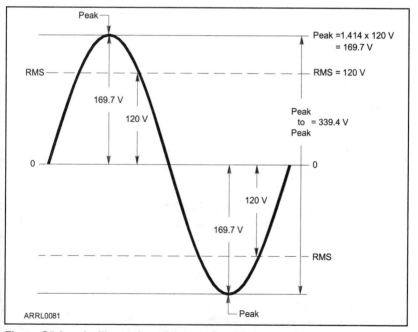

**Figure G5.3 — An illustration of the relationship between ac measurements for sine wave waveforms. RMS value conversions assume that the waveform is a sine wave. Different conversion values are required for other waveform shapes, such as square or triangle waves.**

**G5B10** **What percentage of power loss would result from a transmission line loss of 1 dB?**

A. 10.9 percent
B. 12.2 percent
C. 20.6 percent
D. 25.9 percent

**(C)** See also G5B01. In this question we are told that the transmission line to an antenna results in a signal loss of 1 dB. We can use the decibel equation to calculate the power that reaches the antenna through this feed line, and from that we can calculate the power lost in the feed line. If we assume a transmitter power of 100 W, then the answer will be the percentage of the original power that is lost in the feed line. First, we will solve the decibel equation for $P_2$, the power that reaches the antenna.

$$dB = 10 \times \log_{10}\left(\frac{P_2}{P_1}\right)$$

$$\frac{dB}{10} = \log_{10}\left(\frac{P_2}{P_1}\right)$$

$$\log_{10}^{-1}\left(\frac{dB}{10}\right) = \left(\frac{P_2}{P_1}\right)$$

$$P_1 \log_{10}^{-1}\left(\frac{dB}{10}\right) = P_2$$

Note: The notation that shows the logarithm raised to the negative 1 power means the antilog, or inverse logarithm. On some scientific calculators this button is also labeled $10^x$, which means "raise 10 to the power of this value." The decibel value is given as a loss of 1 dB, so we will write that as −1 dB.

$$100\,\text{W} \times \log_{10}^{-1}\left(\frac{-1\,dB}{10}\right) = 100\,\text{W} \times 0.794 = 79.4\,\text{W}$$

If 79.4 W is the power actually reaching the antenna, then we can calculate the lost power by subtracting this value from the original power: 100 W − 79.4 W = 20.6 W.

Because we used 100 W as the reference power, this value is the percentage of the original power that is lost in our feed line, when it has a loss of 1 dB. The percentage of the power lost in this feed line is 20.6%.

[*General Class License Manual*, page 4-3]

**G5B11** **What is the ratio of peak envelope power to average power for an unmodulated carrier?**

A. 0.707
B. 1.00
C. 1.414
D. 2.00

**(B)** The ratio is 1.0 because for an unmodulated carrier all RF cycles have the same voltage, meaning that the envelope's average and peak values are the same. [*General Class License Manual*, page 4-7]

**G5B12** **What would be the RMS voltage across a 50 ohm dummy load dissipating 1200 watts?**

A. 173 volts
B. 245 volts
C. 346 volts
D. 692 volts

**(B)** The voltage is 245 V because $P = E^2 / R$, so $E = \sqrt{1200 \times 50}$. This is the RMS voltage across the 50 ohm load. [*General Class License Manual*, page 4-6]

**G5B13** **What is the output PEP of an unmodulated carrier if an average reading wattmeter connected to the transmitter output indicates 1060 watts?**

A. 530 watts
B. 1060 watts
C. 1500 watts
D. 2120 watts

**(B)** The PEP and average power of an unmodulated carrier are the same. (See also G5B11.) [*General Class License Manual*, page 4-6]

**G5B14** **What is the output PEP from a transmitter if an oscilloscope measures 500 volts peak-to-peak across a 50 ohm resistive load connected to the transmitter output?**

A. 8.75 watts
B. 625 watts
C. 2500 watts
D. 5000 watts

**(B)** $PEP = (E_{RMS})^2 / R = (250 \times 0.707)^2 / 50 = 625$ W [*General Class License Manual*, page 4-6]

# G5C — Resistors, capacitors, and inductors in series and parallel; transformers

**G5C01** **What causes a voltage to appear across the secondary winding of a transformer when an AC voltage source is connected across its primary winding?**

A. Capacitive coupling
B. Displacement current coupling
C. Mutual inductance
D. Mutual capacitance

**(C)** A transformer consists of two coils (windings) sharing a common core so that the flux from current flowing in one winding is shared by both windings (see **Figure G5.4**). When current flows through the primary winding it creates a magnetic field in the core. That magnetic field changes polarity and strength as the primary ac voltage changes. The changing magnetic field in the common core is shared by the secondary winding, inducing a voltage across the turns of the secondary winding and creating a current in the secondary circuit. The core material might be layers of steel, a powdered iron mixture, some other magnetic material, or even air. The coupling between the primary and secondary windings is called mutual inductance. [*General Class License Manual*, page 4-13]

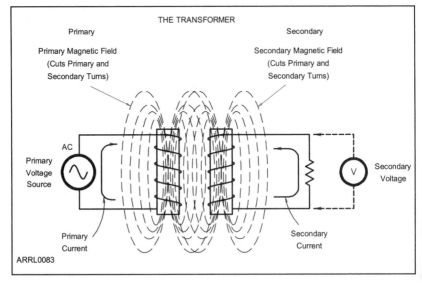

**Figure G5.4 — An illustration of how a transformer works. The input of a transformer is called the primary winding, and the output is called the secondary winding. In this drawing, separate primary and secondary cores are shown to illustrate how the windings share magnetic flux. In most transformers, both windings are wound on a common core for more complete sharing of flux.**

**G5C02** **What happens if a signal is applied to the secondary winding of a 4:1 voltage step-down transformer instead of the primary winding?**

A. The output voltage is multiplied by 4
B. The output voltage is divided by 4
C. Additional resistance must be added in series with the primary to prevent overload
D. Additional resistance must be added in parallel with the secondary to prevent overload

**(A)** The output voltage from the transformer depends on the turns ratio as described in the explanation for question G5C06. If the roles of the primary and secondary windings in transformer with an output voltage less than the input voltage by a factor of 4:1 (step-down) are reversed then the output voltage will be four times higher (step-up). [*General Class License Manual*, page 4-14]

**G5C03** **Which of the following components increases the total resistance of a resistor?**

A. A parallel resistor
B. A series resistor
C. A series capacitor
D. A parallel capacitor

**(B)** Add additional resistors in series to increase the total resistance. [*General Class License Manual*, page 4-15]

**G5C04** **What is the total resistance of three 100 ohm resistors in parallel?**

A. 0.30 ohms
B. 0.33 ohms
C. 33.3 ohms
D. 300 ohms

**(C)** To calculate the total resistance of resistors in parallel take the reciprocal of the sum of the resistor's reciprocal values as follows:

$$R = \frac{1}{\dfrac{1}{100} + \dfrac{1}{100} + \dfrac{1}{100}} = \frac{100}{3} = 33.3 \ \Omega$$

[*General Class License Manual*, page 4-17]

**G5C05**  **If three equal value resistors in series produce 450 ohms, what is the value of each resistor?**

A.  1500 ohms
B.  90 ohms
C.  150 ohms
D.  175 ohms

**(C)**    For N resistors in series, resulting equivalent resistance equals the sum of the resistor values. If the resistors all share an equal common value the calculation can be simplified to:

R = R1 + R2 + R3 +... = Common value × N.

In series, the total resistance of 450 Ω = Common Value × 3. The common value can be calculated from either equation:

Common value = 3 × 50 = 150 Ω or Common value = 450 / 3 = 150 Ω.

[*General Class License Manual*, page 4-17]

**G5C06**  **What is the RMS voltage across a 500-turn secondary winding in a transformer if the 2250-turn primary is connected to 120 VAC?**

A.  2370 volts
B.  540 volts
C.  26.7 volts
D.  5.9 volts

**(C)**    The voltage in the secondary winding of a transformer is equal to the voltage in the primary winding times the turns ratio of windings in the secondary to the primary.

$$E_S = E_P \times \text{Turns ratio} = E_P \times \frac{N_S}{N_P}$$

Since the amount of power going in and out of the transformer is the same, if voltage goes up, current must go down by the same amount:

$$I_S = I_P \times \frac{1}{\text{Turns ratio}} = I_P \times \frac{N_P}{N_S}$$

If the 2250-turn primary is connected to 120 volts ac, the voltage across a 500-turn secondary winding in the transformer is 26.7 volts:

$$E_S = 120\,\text{V} \times \frac{500}{2250} = 26.7\,\text{V}$$

[*General Class License Manual*, page 4-14]

**G5C07**     **What is the turns ratio of a transformer used to match an audio amplifier having 600 ohm output impedance to a speaker having 4 ohm impedance?**

A.  12.2 to 1
B.  24.4 to 1
C.  150 to 1
D.  300 to 1

**(A)**     See G5C06. Because the transformer changes the ratio of both voltage and current between the primary and secondary, the ratio of primary and secondary impedances are controlled by the square of the turns ratio:

$$Z_{PRI} = Z_{SEC}\left(\frac{N_P}{N_S}\right)^2 \text{ and } \frac{N_P}{N_S} = \sqrt{\frac{Z_{PRI}}{Z_{SEC}}}$$

To calculate the required turns ratio:

$$\frac{N_P}{N_S} = \sqrt{\frac{600}{4}} = \sqrt{125} = 12.2$$

[*General Class License Manual*, page 4-22]

**G5C08**     **What is the equivalent capacitance of two 5.0 nanofarad capacitors and one 750 picofarad capacitor connected in parallel?**

A.  576.9 nanofarads
B.  1733 picofarads
C.  3583 picofarads
D.  10,750 nanofarads

**(D)**     To calculate the total capacitance of capacitors in parallel add the values of the capacitors together,

C = C1 + C2 + C3 + …

In this case:

C = 5.0 nF + 5.0 nF + 750 pF = 5000 pF + 5000 pF + 750 pF = 10,750 pF

[*General Class License Manual*, page 4-17]

**G5C09** **What is the capacitance of three 100 microfarad capacitors connected in series?**

A. 0.30 microfarads
B. 0.33 microfarads
C. 33.3 microfarads
D. 300 microfarads

**(C)** For N capacitors with an equal common value in series, the resulting capacitance equals the common capacitor value divided by the number of capacitors,

C = Common value / N

C = 100 μF / 3 = 33.3 μF

[*General Class License Manual*, page 4-17]

**G5C10** **What is the inductance of three 10 millihenry inductors connected in parallel?**

A. 0.30 henries
B. 3.3 henries
C. 3.3 millihenries
D. 30 millihenries

**(C)** For N inductors with an equal common value in parallel, the resulting inductance equals the common inductor value divided by the number of inductors,

L = Common value / N

L = 10 mH / 3 = 3.3 mH

[*General Class License Manual*, page 4-17]

**G5C11** **What is the inductance of a 20 millihenry inductor connected in series with a 50 millihenry inductor?**

A. 0.07 millihenries
B. 14.3 millihenries
C. 70 millihenries
D. 1000 millihenries

**(C)** To calculate the total inductance in series and add the values of the inductors together,

L = L1 + L2 + L3 +...

L = 20 mH + 50 mH = 70 mH

[*General Class License Manual*, page 4-17]

**G5C12** **What is the capacitance of a 20 microfarad capacitor connected in series with a 50 microfarad capacitor?**

A. 0.07 microfarads
B. 14.3 microfarads
C. 70 microfarads
D. 1000 microfarads

**(B)** To calculate the total capacitance of capacitors in series take the reciprocal of the sum of the capacitor's reciprocal values as follows:

$$C = \cfrac{1}{\cfrac{1}{C_1} + \cfrac{1}{C_2} + \cdots + \cfrac{1}{C_N}}$$

In the case of two capacitors in series, the equation simplifies to:

$$C = \frac{C_1 \times C_2}{C_1 + C_2} = \frac{20 \times 50}{20 + 50} = \frac{1000}{70} = 14.3 \ \mu F$$

[*General Class License Manual*, page 4-17]

**G5C13** **Which of the following components should be added to a capacitor to increase the capacitance?**

A. An inductor in series
B. A resistor in series
C. A capacitor in parallel
D. A capacitor in series

**(C)** Add additional capacitors in parallel to increase the total capacitance. [*General Class License Manual*, page 4-15]

**G5C14** **Which of the following components should be added to an inductor to increase the inductance?**

A. A capacitor in series
B. A resistor in parallel
C. An inductor in parallel
D. An inductor in series

**(D)** Add additional inductors in series to increase the total inductance. [*General Class License Manual*, page 4-15]

**G5C15** **What is the total resistance of a 10 ohm, a 20 ohm, and a 50 ohm resistor connected in parallel?**

A. 5.9 ohms
B. 0.17 ohms
C. 10,000 ohms
D. 80 ohms

**(A)** To calculate the total resistance of resistors in parallel take the reciprocal of the sum of the resistor's reciprocal values as follows:

$$R = \frac{1}{\dfrac{1}{10} + \dfrac{1}{20} + \dfrac{1}{50}} = 5.9\ \Omega$$

[*General Class License Manual*, page 4-17]

**G5C16** **Why is the conductor of the primary winding of many voltage step-up transformers larger in diameter than the conductor of the secondary winding?**

A. To improve the coupling between the primary and secondary
B. To accommodate the higher current of the primary
C. To prevent parasitic oscillations due to resistive losses in the primary
D. To ensure that the volume of the primary winding is equal to the volume of the secondary winding

**(B)** See G5C06. To carry a certain amount of current without overheating from resistance, transformer winding wire has a minimum size. If the voltage is stepped-up from primary to secondary, the secondary current will be smaller than the primary current. That means the wire in the secondary winding can be smaller in diameter without having excessive heating. [*General Class License Manual*, page 4-14]

**G5C17** **What is the value in nanofarads (nF) of a 22,000 picofarad (pF) capacitor?**

A. 0.22
B. 2.2
C. 22
D. 220

**(C)** To convert from nanofarads ($10^{-9}$ F) to picofarads ($10^{-12}$ F), divide the value by 1000. [*General Class License Manual*, page 4-13]

**G5C18** **What is the value in microfarads of a 4700 nanofarad (nF) capacitor?**

A. 47
B. 0.47
C. 47,000
D. 4.7

**(D)** To convert from microfarads ($10^{-6}$ F) to nanofarads ($10^{-9}$ F), divide the value by 1000. [*General Class License Manual*, page 4-13]

# Circuit Components

Your General class exam (Element 3) will consist of 35 questions taken from the General class question pool as prepared by the Volunteer Examiner Coordinators' Question Pool Committee. A certain number of questions are taken from each of the 10 subelements. There will be 2 questions from the subelement shown in this chapter. These questions are divided into 2 groups, labeled G6A and G6B.

## SUBELEMENT G6 — CIRCUIT COMPONENTS
### [2 Exam Questions — 2 Groups]

### G6A — Resistors; capacitors; inductors; rectifiers; solid-state diodes and transistors; vacuum tubes; batteries

**G6A01**   **What is the minimum allowable discharge voltage for maximum life of a standard 12 volt lead-acid battery?**

A.   6 volts
B.   8.5 volts
C.   10.5 volts
D.   12 volts

**(C)**   Standard 12-volt lead-acid batteries are composed of six 2-volt cells connected in series. Each cell should not be discharged below 1.75 volts to avoid causing irreversible chemical changes that damage the cell. Thus, the minimum voltage for a standard 12-volt battery is 6 × 1.75 = 10.5 volts. [*General Class License Manual*, page 4-36]

**G6A02**   **What is an advantage of the low internal resistance of nickel-cadmium batteries?**

A.   Long life
B.   High discharge current
C.   High voltage
D.   Rapid recharge

**(B)**   Nickel-cadmium (NiCd) batteries can supply large quantities of current very quickly. This makes them useful in portable power tools and radio transceivers. [*General Class License Manual*, page 4-36]

**G6A03** **What is the approximate junction threshold voltage of a germanium diode?**

A. 0.1 volt
B. 0.3 volts
C. 0.7 volts
D. 1.0 volts

**(B)**    The junction threshold voltage is the voltage at which a diode begins to conduct significant current across its PN junction. The amount of voltage depends on the material from which the diode is constructed. The junction threshold voltage of silicon diodes is approximately 0.7 V and for germanium diodes approximately 0.3 V. [*General Class License Manual*, page 4-24]

**G6A04** **Which of the following is an advantage of an electrolytic capacitor?**

A. Tight tolerance
B. Much less leakage than any other type
C. High capacitance for a given volume
D. Inexpensive RF capacitor

**(C)**    Electrolytic capacitors are designed to provide large values of capacitance for energy storage and ac voltage filtering. Their construction, shown in **Figure G6.1**, provides relatively high capacitance in a small volume at low cost. The tradeoff is that dc voltage applied to them must always be of the same polarity, current leaks through them in relatively high amounts, and the manufacturing technique used to make them leads to rather wide variations in capacitance. [*General Class License Manual*, page 4-12]

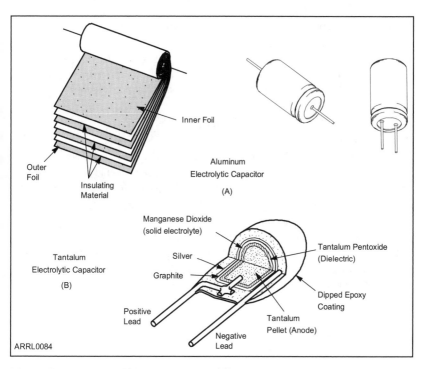

Figure G6.1 — Part A shows the construction of an aluminum electrolytic capacitor. Part B shows the construction of a tantalum electrolytic capacitor.

**G6A05** What is the approximate junction threshold voltage of a conventional silicon diode?

A. 0.1 volt
B. 0.3 volts
C. 0.7 volts
D. 1.0 volts

**(C)** See G6A03 [*General Class License Manual*, page 5-24]

**G6A06** **Which of the following is a reason not to use wire-wound resistors in an RF circuit?**

A. The resistor's tolerance value would not be adequate for such a circuit

B. The resistor's inductance could make circuit performance unpredictable

C. The resistor could overheat

D. The resistor's internal capacitance would detune the circuit

**(B)** Wire-wound resistors are made exactly as their name implies: A length of wire made from a metallic alloy with high resistance is wound around a ceramic form to reduce the overall length of the resistor. The resistor is then coated with a ceramic or other insulating material to protect the wire. If this construction method sounds like an inductor to you, you are absolutely correct! It is not a good idea to use wire-wound resistors in any RF circuits or anywhere you don't want some extra amount of inductance to be included in the circuit. The extra inductance will detune any resonant circuit to which it is connected or add unwanted inductive reactance to signal paths. [*General Class License Manual*, page 4-21]

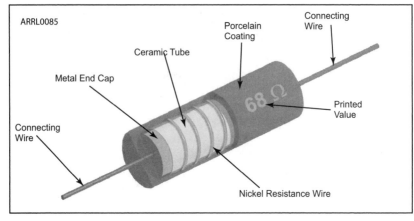

**Figure G6.2 — This drawing shows the construction of a simple wire-wound resistor.**

**G6A07**   **What are the stable operating points for a bipolar transistor used as a switch in a logic circuit?**

A. Its saturation and cutoff regions
B. Its active region (between the cutoff and saturation regions)
C. Its peak and valley current points
D. Its enhancement and depletion modes

**(A)**      When a bipolar transistor is used as a switch in a logic circuit it is important that the switch either be "all the way on" or "all the way off." This is achieved by operating the transistor either in its saturation region to turn the switch on, or in its cut-off region to turn the switch off. [*General Class License Manual*, page 4-25]

**G6A08**   **What is an advantage of using a ferrite core toroidal inductor?**

A. Large values of inductance may be obtained
B. The magnetic properties of the core may be optimized for a specific range of frequencies
C. Most of the magnetic field is contained in the core
D. All these choices are correct

**(D)**      Because a toroid core offers a continuous, circular path for magnetic flux, nearly all of a toroidal inductor's magnetic field is contained inside the core. This gives toroidal inductors a self-shielding property that makes them ideal for use in RF circuits, where interaction between nearby inductors is undesirable. Ferrite is a ceramic containing magnetic compounds. Ferrite and powdered-iron toroid cores both have high permeabilities (the ability to store magnetic energy) and make it possible to obtain large values of inductance in a relatively small package, compared to an air-core inductor. Toroid cores are made from different mixes (types of material) that are optimized for use in specific frequency ranges. [*General Class License Manual*, page 4-12]

**G6A09**   **Which of the following describes the construction of a MOSFET?**

A. The gate is formed by a back-biased junction
B. The gate is separated from the channel with a thin insulating layer
C. The source is separated from the drain by a thin insulating layer
D. The source is formed by depositing metal on silicon

**(B)**      A MOSFET (Metal Oxide Semiconductor Field Effect Transistor) is similar to a JFET (Junction Field Effect Transistor), but instead of the gate electrode being in direct contact with the channel between drain and source, it is insulated by a thin insulating layer of oxide. The gate voltage still controls electron flow between the drain and source, but very little current flows in the gate circuit. [*General Class License Manual*, page 4-25]

**G6A10** **Which element of a triode vacuum tube is used to regulate the flow of electrons between cathode and plate?**

A. Control grid
B. Heater
C. Screen grid
D. Trigger electrode

**(A)** The control grid is closest to the cathode, the element of the tube that generates the electrons. By varying the control grid voltage with respect to the cathode voltage, electron flow between cathode and plate can be controlled. [*General Class License Manual*, page 4-26]

**G6A11** **What happens when an inductor is operated above its self-resonant frequency?**

A. Its reactance increases
B. Harmonics are generated
C. It becomes capacitive
D. Catastrophic failure is likely

**(C)** Resonance can also occur when a component's expected reactance is equal to the reactance of its parasitic reactance. This is called self-resonance. The result is a component that appears to be a short- or open-circuit at the self-resonant frequency. Above the self-resonant frequency, the component's reactance switches type, making an inductor capacitive and a capacitor inductive. [*General Class License Manual*, page 4-22]

**G6A12** **What is the primary purpose of a screen grid in a vacuum tube?**

A. To reduce grid-to-plate capacitance
B. To increase efficiency
C. To increase the control grid resistance
D. To decrease plate resistance

**(A)** The screen grid is placed between the plate and control grid and kept at a constant voltage. This isolates the control grid from the plate and reduces the capacitance between them. [*General Class License Manual*, page 4-26]

**G6A13** **Why is the polarity of applied voltages important for polarized capacitors?**

A. Incorrect polarity can cause the capacitor to short-circuit
B. Reverse voltages can destroy the dielectric layer of an electrolytic capacitor
C. The capacitor could overheat and explode
D. All these choices are correct

**(D)** Polarized capacitors are designed to withstand an applied voltage of a specific polarity. Applying voltage with the reverse polarity can cause the dielectric in the capacitor to break down, leading to short-circuits and excess heat and gas inside the capacitor which can rupture the capacitor's outside case or coating. Some capacitors designed for high-voltage or connection to the ac line are polarized to prevent hazardous voltages from appearing on the capacitor's case or outer layer. [*General Class License Manual*, page 4-12]

**G6A14** **Which of the following is an advantage of ceramic capacitors as compared to other types of capacitors?**

A. Tight tolerance
B. High stability
C. High capacitance for given volume
D. Comparatively low cost

**(D)** The primary advantage of ceramic capacitors is that they offer good performance at low cost. Ceramic capacitors are usually used as bypass capacitors to filter out high-frequency ac voltages from dc and low-frequency signal connections. [*General Class License Manual*, page 4-13]

## G6B — Analog and digital integrated circuits (ICs); microprocessors; memory; I/O devices; microwave ICs (MMICs); display devices; connectors; ferrite cores

**G6B01** **What determines the performance of a ferrite core at different frequencies?**

A. Its conductivity
B. Its thickness
C. The composition, or "mix," of materials used
D. The ratio of outer diameter to inner diameter

**(C)** Toroids may be wound on ferrite or powdered iron cores. (Ferrite is a ceramic containing iron compounds.) These cores make it possible to obtain large values of inductance in a relatively small package compared to using an air core. The combination of materials (or mix) used to make the core is selected so the inductor performs best over a specific range of frequencies. [*General Class License Manual*, page 4-12]

**G6B02    What is meant by the term MMIC?**

A. Multi-Megabyte Integrated Circuit
B. Monolithic Microwave Integrated Circuit
C. Military Manufactured Integrated Circuit
D. Mode Modulated Integrated Circuit

**(B)**    An MMIC is a special type of analog IC containing circuits to perform RF operations such as amplification, modulation and demodulation, and mixing at HF through microwave frequencies. Some MMICs combine several functions, acting as an entire receiver front end, for example. The MMIC is what enables communications engineers to construct low-cost, hand-held mobile phones and GPS receivers, among other sophisticated examples of wireless technology. [*General Class License Manual*, page 4-30]

**G6B03    Which of the following is an advantage of CMOS integrated circuits compared to TTL integrated circuits?**

A. Low power consumption
B. High power handling capability
C. Better suited for RF amplification
D. Better suited for power supply regulation

**(A)**    Integrated circuits based on CMOS (Complementary Metal Oxide Semiconductor) technology consume very little current when operating, only drawing significant power when switching between ON and OFF states. [*General Class License Manual*, page 4-28]

**G6B04    What is meant by the term ROM?**

A. Resistor Operated Memory
B. Read Only Memory
C. Random Operational Memory
D. Resistant to Overload Memory

**(B)**    ROM, or read-only memory, contains data or program instructions that do not need to be changed. [*General Class License Manual*, page 4-30]

**G6B05    What is meant when memory is characterized as non-volatile?**

A. It is resistant to radiation damage
B. It is resistant to high temperatures
C. The stored information is maintained even if power is removed
D. The stored information cannot be changed once written

**(C)**    Non-volatile memory can retain stored data even if power is removed and restored. It never needs to have the data "refreshed." Volatile memory loses the data if power is removed and often needs to have the data refreshed while in operation, such as for dynamic types of memory. [*General Class License Manual*, page 4-30]

**G6B06** **What kind of device is an integrated circuit operational amplifier?**

A. Digital
B. MMIC
C. Programmable Logic
D. Analog

**(D)** An operational amplifier, or op amp, is an analog circuit, operating over a continuous range of voltage and current. [*General Class License Manual*, page 4-27]


**G6B07** **Which of the following describes a type N connector?**

A. A moisture-resistant RF connector useful to 10 GHz
B. A small bayonet connector used for data circuits
C. A threaded connector used for hydraulic systems
D. An audio connector used in surround-sound installations

**(A)** Type N connectors are connectors for coaxial cable used at HF, VHF, UHF and microwave frequencies up to 10 GHz. The type N connector shell is threaded like a PL-259, but the special design of the connector body presents the same 50-Ω impedance as coaxial cable so no signal energy is reflected at the junction of connector and feed line. Type N connectors also have special gaskets built-in so that they are waterproof without requiring additional coatings. [*General Class License Manual*, page 4-40]


**G6B08** **How is an LED biased when emitting light?**

A. Beyond cutoff
B. At the Zener voltage
C. Reverse biased
D. Forward biased

**(D)** A forward biased LED emits light when current flows through the PN-junction of the diode. Photons are given off when the electrons from the N-type material combine with the holes in the P-type material. [*General Class License Manual*, page 4-31]

**G6B09** **Which of the following is a characteristic of a liquid crystal display?**

    A. It utilizes ambient or back lighting
    B. It offers a wide dynamic range
    C. It consumes relatively high power
    D. It has relatively short lifetime

**(A)**    A liquid crystal display (LCD) works by blocking the transmission of light through an otherwise transparent layer of liquid crystals. Transparent electrodes are printed on the glass layers on either side of the liquid crystals to form the pattern of the digits, characters, and symbols. When voltage of the right polarity is applied between the electrodes, the liquid crystals twist into a pattern that blocks light. This is why an LCD requires ambient light to reflect off the back of the display or an active source of light behind the liquid crystals (backlighting) in order to see the desired pattern. [*General Class License Manual*, page 4-31]

**G6B10** **How does a ferrite bead or core reduce common-mode RF current on the shield of a coaxial cable?**

    A. By creating an impedance in the current's path
    B. It converts common-mode current to differential mode
    C. By creating an out-of-phase current to cancel the common-mode current
    D. Ferrites expel magnetic fields

**(A)**    A common approach to cure RFI is to block RF current flow by placing an impedance in its path. This is done by forming the conductor carrying the RF current into an RF choke by winding it around or through a ferrite core. [*General Class License Manual*, page 5-24]

**G6B11** **What is a type SMA connector?**

    A. A large bayonet connector usable at power levels more than 1 kW
    B. A small threaded connector suitable for signals up to several GHz
    C. A connector designed for serial multiple access signals
    D. A type of push-on connector intended for high-voltage applications

**(B)**    SMA connectors are small threaded connectors designed for miniature coaxial cable and are rated for use up to 18 GHz. Handheld transceivers often use SMA connectors for attaching antennas. [*General Class License Manual*, page 4-40]

**G6B12** Which of these connector types is commonly used for audio signals in Amateur Radio stations?

    A. PL-259
    B. BNC
    C. RCA Phono
    D. Type N

**(C)** The RCA phono connector is the most common audio signal connector for consumer electronics and a great deal of amateur equipment. The connector's name derives from its early use by the RCA Company for audio connectors and its subsequent popularity for the connection of phonographs to amplifiers and receivers. [*General Class License Manual*, page 4-38]

**G6B13** Which of these connector types is commonly used for RF connections at frequencies up to 150 MHz?

    A. Octal
    B. RJ-11
    C. PL-259
    D. DB-25

**(C)** The UHF connector family includes the PL-259 cable plug and SO-239 chassis-mounted receptacle. It is the most popular type of RF connector used on amateur equipment. UHF does not refer to a frequency range in this case. [*General Class License Manual*, page 4-39]

Figure G6.3 — This photo shows some common coaxial-cable connectors. At left is a BNC connector pair. They are a popular connector for RG-58-size cable. In the center is a pair of type N connectors. These are often used for UHF equipment because of their low loss. Type N connectors provide a weatherproof connector for RG-213-size cables. At the right is a PL-259 coaxial connector and its mating SO-239 chassis connector. Most HF equipment uses these connectors. They are designed for use with RG-213-size cables, although reducing adapters are available for smaller-diameter cables such as RG-58 and RG-59. Although the PL-259 is called a "UHF connector," in this case UHF does not refer to a frequency range.

# Practical Circuits

Your General class exam (Element 3) will consist of 35 questions taken from the General class question pool as prepared by the Volunteer Examiner Coordinators' Question Pool Committee. A certain number of questions are taken from each of the 10 subelements. There will be 3 questions from the subelement shown in this chapter. These questions are divided into 3 groups, labeled G7A through G7C.

## SUBELEMENT G7 — PRACTICAL CIRCUITS
### [3 Exam Questions — 3 Groups]

### G7A — Power supplies; schematic symbols

**G7A01** **What useful feature does a power supply bleeder resistor provide?**

A. It acts as a fuse for excess voltage
B. It ensures that the filter capacitors are discharged when power is removed
C. It removes shock hazards from the induction coils
D. It eliminates ground loop current

**(B)**    After power is turned off, the power supply filter capacitor in **Figure G7.1** cannot discharge back through the rectifier circuit, so it could remain charged for a long time. The bleeder resistor slowly discharges the capacitor, minimizing the risk of electrical shock if the supply enclosure is opened, exposing the capacitor terminals. [*General Class License Manual*, page 4-33]

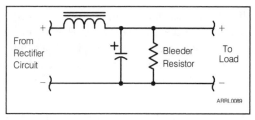

**Figure G7.1 — A bleeder resistor is a safety feature that discharges a power supply filter capacitor when the supply is turned off.**

**G7A02** Which of the following components are used in a power supply filter network?

A. Diodes
B. Transformers and transducers
C. Quartz crystals
D. Capacitors and inductors

**(D)** A power supply filter network consists of capacitors and sometimes inductors. It is used to smooth out the pulses of voltage and current from the rectifier. Capacitors oppose changes in voltage while the inductors oppose changes in current. The combination results in a constant dc output voltage from the supply. Most power supply filters consist solely of capacitors. Inductors are generally added in high-voltage, low-current supplies. See **Figure G7.2**. [*General Class License Manual*, page 4-33]

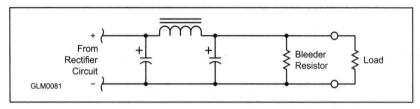

Figure G7.2 — A capacitor-input power supply filter circuit. A choke inductor and second capacitor are sometimes used in high voltage (HV) supplies for RF power amplifiers.

**G7A03** Which type of rectifier circuit uses two diodes and a center-tapped transformer?

A. Full-wave
B. Full-wave bridge
C. Half-wave
D. Synchronous

**(B)** The full-wave rectifier shown in **Figure G7.3B** is really two half-wave rectifiers operating on alternate half-cycles. This rectifier requires that the transformer output winding be center-tapped to provide a return path for current that flows in the load. [*General Class License Manual*, page 4-32]

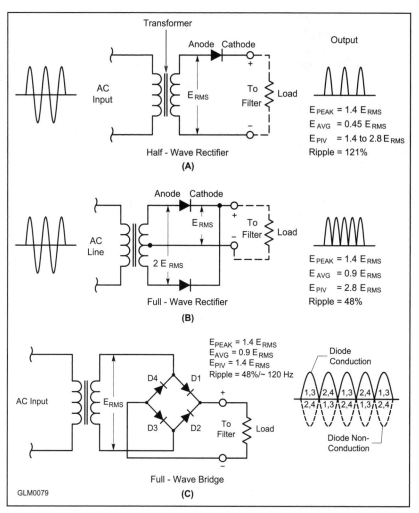

**Figure G7.3 — Three fundamental rectifier circuits and the characteristics of their output voltage. (A) Half-wave. (B) Full-wave center-tapped. (C) Full-wave bridge. The half-wave rectifier circuit converts only one-half of the input waveform cycle (180°) while the full-wave circuits convert the entire cycle (360°). In most power supplies, a capacitor is connected across the output of the rectifier and will charge to a voltage of $E_{PEAK}$, the normal peak output of the supply.**

**G7A04** **What is an advantage of a half-wave rectifier in a power supply?**

A. Only one diode is required
B. The ripple frequency is twice that of a full-wave rectifier
C. More current can be drawn from the half-wave rectifier
D. The output voltage is two times the peak output voltage of the transformer

**(A)** The half-wave rectifier shown in **Figure G7.3A** uses only one diode that permits current flow during one-half of the input ac waveform (180°) from the transformer. [*General Class License Manual*, page 4-32]

**G7A05** **What portion of the AC cycle is converted to DC by a half-wave rectifier?**

A. 90 degrees
B. 180 degrees
C. 270 degrees
D. 360 degrees

**(B)** Since there are 360 degrees in a full cycle of ac, a half-wave rectifier converts 180 degrees of the ac input waveform to dc. [*General Class License Manual*, page 4-32]

**G7A06** **What portion of the AC cycle is converted to DC by a full-wave rectifier?**

A. 90 degrees
B. 180 degrees
C. 270 degrees
D. 360 degrees

**(D)** Since there are 360 degrees in a full cycle of ac, a full-wave rectifier converts 360 degrees of the ac input waveform to dc. [*General Class License Manual*, page 4-32]

**G7A07**   **What is the output waveform of an unfiltered full-wave rectifier connected to a resistive load?**

A. A series of DC pulses at twice the frequency of the AC input
B. A series of DC pulses at the same frequency as the AC input
C. A sine wave at half the frequency of the AC input
D. A steady DC voltage

**(A)**   A full-wave rectifier changes alternating current with positive and negative half cycles into a fluctuating current with all positive pulses. Since the current has not been filtered, it is a series of pulses at twice the frequency of the ac input. [*General Class License Manual*, page 4-32]

**G7A08**   **Which of the following is an advantage of a switchmode power supply as compared to a linear power supply?**

A. Faster switching time makes higher output voltage possible
B. Fewer circuit components are required
C. High-frequency operation allows the use of smaller components
D. All these choices are correct

**(C)**   Switchmode power supplies operate by converting ac to dc at a high frequency: 50 kHz or more is common. This allows the use of small, lightweight transformers. While the transformer in a linear power supply capable of supplying 20 amperes might weigh 15 or 20 pounds, the transformer for a switchmode power supply with a similar current rating might weigh 1 or 2 pounds! Switchmode power supplies have more complex circuits than linear supplies and generally require more components than a simple linear supply. [*General Class License Manual*, page 4-33]

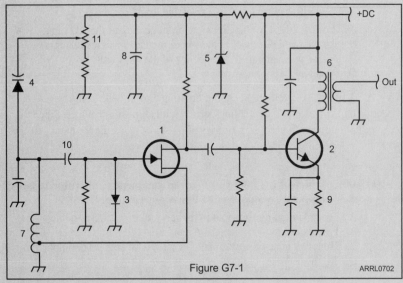

Figure G7-1

ARRL0702

**Question Pool Figure G7-1 — This schematic is used in General class exam for questions G7A09 to G7A13.**

    **G7A09**    **Which symbol in figure G7-1 represents a field effect transistor?**

    A. Symbol 2
    B. Symbol 5
    C. Symbol 1
    D. Symbol 4

**(C)**    [*General Class License Manual*, page 4-7]

**G7A10    Which symbol in figure G7-1 represents a Zener diode?**
A. Symbol 4
B. Symbol 1
C. Symbol 11
D. Symbol 5

**(D)**    [*General Class License Manual*, page 4-7]


**G7A11    Which symbol in figure G7-1 represents an NPN junction transistor?**
A. Symbol 1
B. Symbol 2
C. Symbol 7
D. Symbol 11

**(B)**    [*General Class License Manual*, page 4-7]


**G7A12    Which symbol in Figure G7-1 represents a solid core transformer?**
A. Symbol 4
B. Symbol 7
C. Symbol 6
D. Symbol 1

**(C)**    [*General Class License Manual*, page 4-7]


**G7A13    Which symbol in Figure G7-1 represents a tapped inductor?**
A. Symbol 7
B. Symbol 11
C. Symbol 6
D. Symbol 1

**(A)**    [*General Class License Manual*, page 4-7]

# G7B — Digital circuits; amplifiers and oscillators

**G7B01** What is the reason for neutralizing the final amplifier stage of a transmitter?

- A. To limit the modulation index
- B. To eliminate self-oscillations
- C. To cut off the final amplifier during standby periods
- D. To keep the carrier on frequency

**(B)** Neutralization of a power amplifier is a technique that minimizes or cancels the effects of positive feedback. Positive feedback occurs when the output signal is fed back to the input in phase with the input signal, creating an oscillator. This self-oscillation creates powerful spurious signals that cause interference. Self-oscillations can also be sufficiently powerful to damage the amplifier. Neutralization consists of feeding a portion of the amplifier output back to the input, 180 degrees out of phase with the input. This is called negative feedback. Neutralization eliminates self-oscillation by canceling the positive feedback. See **Figure G7.4**. [*General Class License Manual*, page 5-15]

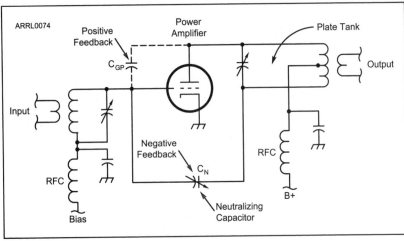

Figure G7.4 — The schematic circuit for a vacuum-tube RF power amplifier shows both the source of positive feedback that can create self-oscillation and negative feedback that cancels or neutralizes the positive feedback. Positive feedback is created by the capacitance from the plate to the grid, shows as $C_{GP}$ on the schematic. The amount of capacitance is small, so the frequency of self-oscillation is usually at VHF or in the upper HF range. Capacitor $C_N$ is connected to a point in the output circuit at which the signal has the opposite phase, so the feedback to the grid acts as negative feedback by providing an equal-and-opposite feedback signal to that from $C_{GP}$.

**G7B02**     **Which of these classes of amplifiers has the highest efficiency?**
   A.  Class A
   B.  Class B
   C.  Class AB
   D.  Class C

**(D)**     Class C amplifiers act a lot like switches — they turn on for a fraction of the input signal's cycle and stay off the rest of the time. While these amplifiers are not linear at all and require filters to reduce the harmonics in their output, they are quite efficient. [*General Class License Manual*, page 5-14]

**G7B03** **Which of the following describes the function of a two-input AND gate?**

A. Output is high when either or both inputs are low
B. Output is high only when both inputs are high
C. Output is low when either or both inputs are high
D. Output is low only when both inputs are high

**(B)** In positive-logic circuits, a high voltage represents a "true" or "1" and a low voltage represents "false" or "0". If both inputs to a positive-logic AND gate are true or "1", represented by a high input voltage, the AND function output is also "1", otherwise the output is "0", represented by a low voltage. See **Figure G7.5A**. [*General Class License Manual*, page 4-28]

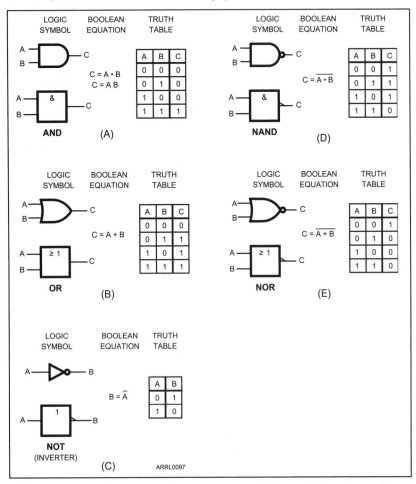

Figure G7.5 — Schematic symbols for the basic digital logic functions with the logic equations and truth tables that describe their operation. The two-input AND gate is shown at A and a two-input NOR gate at E.

**G7B04** **Which of the following describes the function of a two input NOR gate?**

A. Output is high when either or both inputs are low
B. Output is high only when both inputs are high
C. Output is low when either or both inputs are high
D. Output is low only when both inputs are high

**(C)** A NOR (NOT-OR) gate consists of an OR gate with its output inverted. If either or both of the inputs to a positive-logic two-input NOR gate are true or "1", the OR function is also "1", which is then inverted to "0" voltage at the output as shown in **Figure G7.5E**. (See also G7B03.) [*General Class License Manual*, page 4-28]

**G7B05** **How many states does a 3-bit binary counter have?**

A. 3
B. 6
C. 8
D. 16

**(C)** There are 8 states because the number of states in a binary counter is $2^N$, where N is the number of bits in the counter. A 2-bit counter has $2^2 = 4$ states, a 3-bit counter $2^3 = 8$ states, a 4-bit counter $2^4 = 16$ states, and so forth. [*General Class License Manual*, page 4-28]

**G7B06** **What is a shift register?**

A. A clocked array of circuits that passes data in steps along the array
B. An array of operational amplifiers used for tri-state arithmetic operations
C. A digital mixer
D. An analog mixer

**(A)** A shift register consists of a sequence of flip-flop circuits with each output connected to the input of the next stage. All flip-flops share a common clock input signal. With each pulse of the clock signal, the state of the input signal (0 or 1) to the shift register is transferred to the output of the first flip-flop and each subsequent flip-flop's output is passed to the next flip-flop's input, an operation called "shifting." [*General Class License Manual*, page 4-28]

**G7B07** Which of the following are basic components of a sine wave oscillator?

A. An amplifier and a divider
B. A frequency multiplier and a mixer
C. A circulator and a filter operating in a feed-forward loop
D. A filter and an amplifier operating in a feedback loop

**(D)** To make an oscillator requires an amplifier and a circuit to route some of the amplifier's output signal back to the input (called a feedback loop) such that it is reinforced in the amplifier output. This is called positive feedback. A filter in the feedback loop is used so only signals at the desired frequency are reinforced. Starting with random noise, the oscillator gradually builds up an output signal at the filter frequency until it is self-sustaining. [*General Class License Manual,* page 5-4]

**G7B08** How is the efficiency of an RF power amplifier determined?

A. Divide the DC input power by the DC output power
B. Divide the RF output power by the DC input power
C. Multiply the RF input power by the reciprocal of the RF output power
D. Add the RF input power to the DC output power

**(B)** Efficiency is defined as the total output power divided by the total input power and is measured in percent. For an RF amplifier, total output power is measured by a wattmeter. The total input power is the dc power required for the amplifier to operate. For example, if an amplifier requires 1000 mA of plate current at a voltage of 2000 V to produce 1200 watts of RF output, its efficiency = 1200 watts / (1 A × 2000 V) = 1200 / 2000 = 60%. [*General Class License Manual,* page 5-14]

**G7B09** What determines the frequency of an LC oscillator?

A. The number of stages in the counter
B. The number of stages in the divider
C. The inductance and capacitance in the tank circuit
D. The time delay of the lag circuit

**(C)** An LC oscillator uses a parallel LC circuit (a tank circuit, which has that name because it stores energy) as the filter in the feedback loop. (See also G7B07.) [*General Class License Manual,* page 5-4]

**G7B10** **Which of the following describes a linear amplifier?**

A. Any RF power amplifier used in conjunction with an amateur transceiver
B. An amplifier in which the output preserves the input waveform
C. A Class C high efficiency amplifier
D. An amplifier used as a frequency multiplier

**(B)** A linear amplifier is defined as one with an output waveform that is a copy of the input waveform, although larger in amplitude. Hams refer to power amplifiers as "linears", whether they are operating linearly (for AM or SSB modes) or not (for CW or FM). It is important to understand when linear operation is important. An amplifier designed for FM will not be suitable as an SSB amplifier, for example. [*General Class License Manual*, page 5-9]

**G7B11** **For which of the following modes is a Class C power stage appropriate for amplifying a modulated signal?**

A. SSB
B. FM
C. AM
D. All these choices are correct

**(B)** A Class C amplifier conducts current during less than half of the input signal cycle, resulting in high distortion. This rules out Class C amplifiers for any form of amplitude modulation, such as SSB or AM. Class C amplifiers can be used for CW since that mode requires only the presence or absence of a signal. Similarly, Class C is suitable for FM signals that only depend on signal frequency, which is not changed by the amplifier. Class C amplifiers generate significant amounts of harmonic energy, so they require filtering when used as transmitter output stages. [*General Class License Manual*, page 5-14]

# G7C — Receivers and transmitters; filters; oscillators

**G7C01**    Which of the following is used to process signals from the balanced modulator then send them to the mixer in some single sideband phone transmitters?

A.  Carrier oscillator
B.  Filter
C.  IF amplifier
D.  RF amplifier

**(B)**    In a single-sideband transmitter modulating audio can be added to the RF signal by a balanced modulator which also balances out or cancels the original carrier signal. This leaves a double-sideband, suppressed-carrier signal. A filter then removes one of the sidebands, leaving a single-sideband signal that is sent to the mixer, where it combines with the signal from a local oscillator (LO) to produce the RF signal that is amplified and sent to the antenna. The LO shown in the figure is crystal-controlled for fixed-frequency operation. Replacing the crystal-controlled LO with a variable-frequency oscillator (VFO) results in a tunable transmitter similar to those in most modern transceivers. See **Figure G7.6**. [*General Class License Manual*, page 5-9]

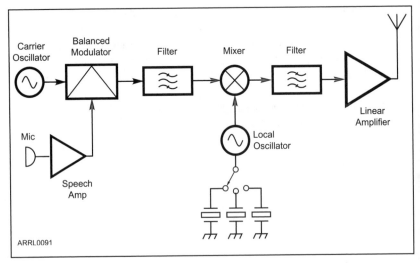

**Figure G7.6 — This block diagram shows a basic single-sideband, suppressed-carrier (SSB) transmitter.**

**G7C02**   **Which circuit is used to combine signals from the carrier oscillator and speech amplifier then send the result to the filter in some single sideband phone transmitters?**

A. Discriminator
B. Detector
C. IF amplifier
D. Balanced modulator

**(D)**   See G7C01. [*General Class License Manual*, page 5-9]

**G7C03**   **What circuit is used to process signals from the RF amplifier and local oscillator then send the result to the IF filter in a superheterodyne receiver?**

A. Balanced modulator
B. IF amplifier
C. Mixer
D. Detector

**(C)**   In a superheterodyne receiver (**Figure G7.7**), the mixer combines signals from the RF amplifier and the local oscillator (LO) then sends those signals to the IF filter, which passes the desired range of frequencies for further amplification while rejecting the signals at higher and lower frequencies. [*General Class License Manual*, page 5-16]

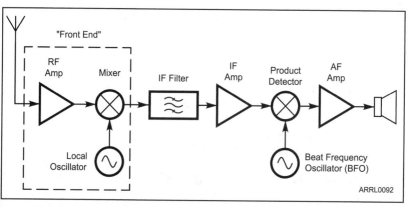

**Figure G7.7 — This block diagram shows a simple superheterodyne SSB receiver.**

**G7C04**  **What circuit is used to combine signals from the IF amplifier and BFO and send the result to the AF amplifier in some single sideband receivers?**

A. RF oscillator
B. IF filter
C. Balanced modulator
D. Product detector

**(D)**   In a superheterodyne receiver, the product detector circuit recovers the modulating audio signal by combining the output of the intermediate frequency (IF) amplifier and the beat frequency oscillator (BFO). The recovered audio signal is then passed to the audio frequency (AF) amplifier. [*General Class License Manual*, page 5-17]

**G7C05**  **Which of the following is an advantage of a direct digital synthesizer (DDS)?**

A. Wide tuning range and no need for band switching
B. Relatively high-power output
C. Relatively low power consumption
D. Variable frequency with the stability of a crystal oscillator

**(D)**   A direct digital synthesizer or DDS replaces analog VFO circuits by creating a sine wave as a series of small steps. The duration and amplitude of each step is precisely controlled and based on a crystal oscillator. This allows a DDS to act as an oscillator with stability that is comparable to that of a crystal oscillator, while still being adjustable over a wide range. [*General Class License Manual*, page 5-5]

**G7C06**  **What should be the impedance of a low-pass filter as compared to the impedance of the transmission line into which it is inserted?**

A. Substantially higher
B. About the same
C. Substantially lower
D. Twice the transmission line impedance

**(B)**   To prevent unwanted reflected power and elevated SWR, keep all elements of the feed line and antenna system at the same impedance. A low-pass filter, designed to be installed at the transmitter output, should have the same impedance as the transmission line. [*General Class License Manual*, page 5-23]

**G7C07** **What is the simplest combination of stages that implement a superheterodyne receiver?**

A. RF amplifier, detector, audio amplifier
B. RF amplifier, mixer, IF discriminator
C. HF oscillator, mixer, detector
D. HF oscillator, prescaler, audio amplifier

**(C)**     By definition, a superheterodyne receiver must contain a mixer and a local oscillator to shift the frequency (heterodyne) of the input signal. One additional stage, a detector, is necessary to recover the modulating audio from the RF signal. Thus, the simplest superheterodyne consists of a mixer, oscillator, and detector. Practical receivers add more amplifiers to improve sensitivity and filters to reject unwanted signals. [*General Class License Manual*, page 5-16]

**G7C08**     **What circuit is used in analog FM receivers to convert IF output signals to audio?**

A. Product detector
B. Phase inverter
C. Mixer
D. Discriminator

**(D)**     A frequency discriminator converts the variations in frequency of the limiter's output signal into amplitude variations, recovering the modulating audio signal. A quadrature detector is another type of FM demodulation circuit that converts changes in frequency into amplitude variations. See **Figure G7.8**. [*General Class License Manual*, page 5-18]

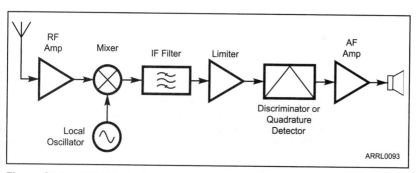

**Figure G7.8 — This block diagram shows a simple FM receiver.**

**G7C09** **What is the phase difference between the I and Q signals that software-defined radio (SDR) equipment uses for modulation and demodulation?**

A. Zero
B. 90 degrees
C. 180 degrees
D. 45 degrees

**(B)**    I refers to in-phase and Q to quadrature. I and Q represent input signals. **Figure G7.9** shows how I/Q modulation works. An RF carrier from a local oscillator (LO) signal is split into two signals, one of which is phase-shifted by 90 degrees. (This is where the word "quadrature" comes from.) The LO signals are applied to a mixer along with the I or Q signal. The result is a pair of modulated signals that are then added together in the combiner stage. The RF output of the combiner consists of a pair of modulated signals that have carrier signals with a 90-degree difference in phase. [*General Class License Manual*, page 5-7]

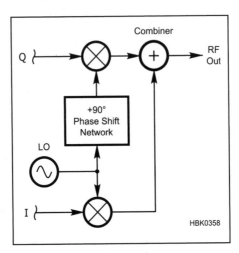

**Figure G7.9 — Block diagram of an I/Q modulator. I and Q are input signals that can be analog signals or streams of digital data.**

**G7C10** **What is an advantage of using I and Q signals in software-defined radios (SDRs)?**

A. The need for high resolution analog-to-digital converters is eliminated
B. All types of modulation can be created with appropriate processing.
C. Minimum detectible signal level is reduced
D. Converting the signal from digital to analog creates mixing products

**(B)** I/Q modulation is primarily used to transmit digital data but different combinations of the I and Q signals can create signals with any type of modulation. [*General Class License Manual*, page 5-7]

**G7C11** **What is meant by the term "software-defined radio" (SDR)?**

A. A radio in which most major signal processing functions are performed by software
B. A radio that provides computer interface for automatic logging of band and frequency
C. A radio that uses crystal filters designed using software
D. A computer model that can simulate performance of a radio to aid in the design process

**(A)** In a software-defined radio (SDR) nearly all of the radio's functions are performed as digital calculations by software. This allows the radio's operation to be changed and controlled by software without having to change the way in which the radio is physically constructed. [*General Class License Manual*, page 5-3]

**G7C12** **What is the frequency above which a low-pass filter's output power is less than half the input power?**

A. Notch frequency
B. Neper frequency
C. Cutoff frequency
D. Rolloff frequency

**(C)** A low-pass filter (**Figure G7.10A**) is one in which all frequencies below the cutoff frequency are passed with little or no attenuation. The cutoff frequency ($f_{co}$) is the frequency at which the output signal power is reduced to one-half that of the input signal. [*General Class License Manual*, page 5-4]

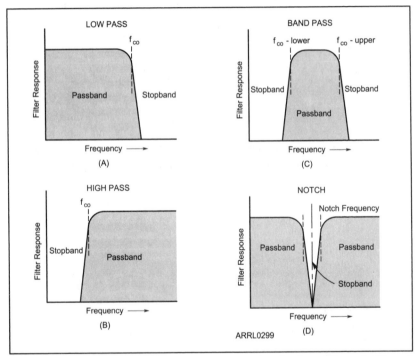

**Figure G7.10 — Generic filter response curves showing how filters of different types affect signals. A larger filter response means less attenuation of the signal. Cutoff frequencies are shown as f$_{co}$.**

**G7C13**    What term specifies a filter's maximum ability to reject signals outside its passband?

A. Notch depth
B. Rolloff
C. Insertion loss
D. Ultimate rejection

**(D)**    Outside the passband, attenuation may vary but the maximum attenuation is the filter's ultimate rejection. [*General Class License Manual*, page 5-4]

**G7C14**    The bandwidth of a band-pass filter is measured between what two frequencies?

A. Upper and lower half-power
B. Cutoff and rolloff
C. Pole and zero
D. Image and harmonic

**(A)**    A band-pass filter (Figure G7.10C) has both an upper and a lower cutoff frequency. Signals between the cutoff frequencies are passed while those outside the passband are attenuated. The frequency range between the upper and lower cutoff frequencies is the filter's bandwidth. [*General Class License Manual*, page 5-4]

**G7C15**    What term specifies a filter's attenuation inside its passband?

A. Insertion loss
B. Return loss
C. Q
D. Ultimate rejection

**(A)**    Even though a filter passes a range of frequencies, it may still attenuate signals in its passband. This is called insertion loss. [*General Class License Manual*, page 5-4]

**G7C16**    Which of the following is a typical application for a Direct Digital Synthesizer?

A. A high-stability variable frequency oscillator in a transceiver
B. A digital voltmeter
C. A digital mode interface between a computer and a transceiver
D. A high-sensitivity radio direction finder

**(A)**    Because their frequency is controlled by a crystal oscillator, DDS oscillators are used as the high-stability VFO in most current transceivers. [*General Class License Manual*, page 5-5]

# Signals and Emissions

Your General class exam (Element 3) will consist of 35 questions taken from the General class question pool as prepared by the Volunteer Examiner Coordinators' Question Pool Committee. A certain number of questions are taken from each of the 10 subelements. There will be 3 questions from the subelement shown in this chapter. These questions are divided into 3 groups, labeled G8A through G8C.

## SUBELEMENT G8 — SIGNALS AND EMISSIONS
## [3 Exam Questions — 3 Groups]

## G8A — Carriers and modulation: AM; FM; single sideband; modulation envelope; digital modulation; overmodulation

**G8A01** How is an FSK signal generated?
A. By keying an FM transmitter with a sub-audible tone
B. By changing an oscillator's frequency directly with a digital control signal
C. By using a transceiver's computer data interface protocol to change frequencies
D. By reconfiguring the CW keying input to act as a tone generator

**(B)** FSK (frequency shift keying) is distinguished from AFSK (audio frequency shift keying) because of the way modulation is performed. AFSK is generated by modulating an SSB transmitter with mark and space audio tones. FSK is often called "direct FSK" to distinguish it from AFSK because a control signal shifts an RF oscillator's frequency with each digital 0 and 1. On the air, properly generated FSK and AFSK are nearly identical. [*General Class License Manual*, page 6-4]

**G8A02** What is the name of the process that changes the phase angle of an RF signal to convey information?

A. Phase convolution
B. Phase modulation
C. Phase transformation
D. Phase inversion

**(B)** There are three characteristics of a sine wave which can be varied in order to carry information as modulation: amplitude, frequency, and phase. Phase modulation varies the phase angle of the sine wave with respect to some reference angle as shown in **Figure G8.1**. [*General Class License Manual*, page 5-2]

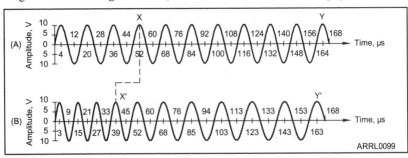

Figure G8.1 — This drawing shows a graphical representation of phase modulation. The unmodulated wave is shown at A. Part B shows the modulated wave. After modulation, cycle X' occurs earlier than cycle X did. All the cycles to the left of X' are compressed, and to the right they are spread out.

**G8A03** What is the name of the process that changes the instantaneous frequency of an RF wave to convey information?

A. Frequency convolution
B. Frequency transformation
C. Frequency conversion
D. Frequency modulation

**(D)** See G8A02 and **Figure G8.2**.
[*General Class License Manual*, page 5-2]

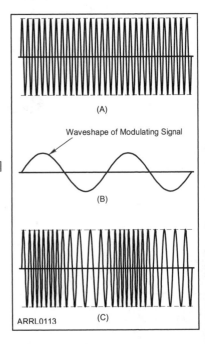

Figure G8.2 — This drawing shows a graphical representation of frequency modulation. In the unmodulated carrier at Part A, each RF cycle takes the same amount of time to complete. When the modulating signal of Part B is applied, the carrier frequency is increased or decreased according to the amplitude and polarity of the modulating signal. Part C shows the modulated RF wave.

**G8A04** **What emission is produced by a reactance modulator connected to a transmitter RF amplifier stage?**

A. Multiplex modulation
B. Phase modulation
C. Amplitude modulation
D. Pulse modulation

**(B)** Reactance modulators are the most common method of generating phase modulation (PM) signals. Phase modulators cause the output signal phase to vary with both the modulating signal's amplitude and frequency. (See also G8A02 and **Figure G8.3**.) [*General Class License Manual*, page 5-7]

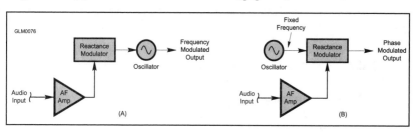

**Figure G8.3 — Reactance modulators can be used to create frequency modulation (A) or phase modulation (B).**

**G8A05** **What type of modulation varies the instantaneous power level of the RF signal?**

A. Frequency shift keying
B. Phase modulation
C. Frequency modulation
D. Amplitude modulation

**(D)** Amplitude modulation (AM) varies the instantaneous amplitude of the RF signal according to the modulating audio signal. (See also G8A02 and **Figure G8.4**.) [*General Class License Manual*, page 5-1]

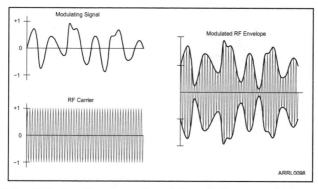

**Figure G8.4 — This drawing shows the relationship between the modulating audio waveform, the RF carrier and the resulting RF envelope in a double-sideband, full-carrier amplitude-modulated signal.**

**G8A06    Which of the following is characteristic of QPSK31?**

    A.  It is sideband sensitive

    B.  Its encoding provides error correction

    C.  Its bandwidth is approximately the same as BPSK31

    D.  All these choices are correct

**(D)**     QPSK31 (quadrature phase shift keying) sends two audio tones so that there are four possible phase shift combinations. That allows data to be encoded in a way that provides some error correction to improve performance in noisy conditions. Since there are two tones, you have to select the right sideband (USB or LSB) to decode the data, meaning the mode is sideband sensitive. QPSK31 and PSK31 have approximately the same bandwidth. [*General Class License Manual*, page 6-5]


**G8A07    Which of the following phone emissions uses the narrowest bandwidth?**

    A.  Single sideband

    B.  Double sideband

    C.  Phase modulation

    D.  Frequency modulation

**(A)**     In a single-sideband (SSB) amplitude-modulated signal, because the carrier and one sideband are removed, only enough bandwidth is required to transmit a single sideband. The bandwidth of an SSB signal is between about 2 and 3 kHz, the bandwidth of a double-sideband AM signal is about 6 kHz and the bandwidth of frequency and phase modulated phone signals is about 16 kHz. [*General Class License Manual*, page 5-2]

### G8A08   Which of the following is an effect of overmodulation?

A. Insufficient audio
B. Insufficient bandwidth
C. Frequency drift
D. Excessive bandwidth

**(D)**   When an SSB signal is overmodulated the output waveform of the signal is distorted, which causes spurious emissions outside the normal bandwidth of the signal (**Figure G8.5**). When an FM or PM signal is overmodulated, the deviation of the signal becomes too high and again, spurious emissions appear outside the normal bandwidth of the signal. In both cases, the spurious emissions can cause interference to other stations. [*General Class License Manual*, page 5-11]

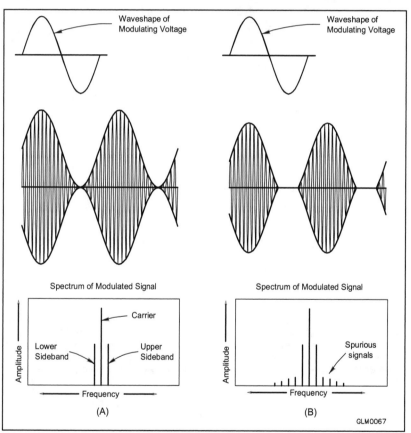

**Figure G8.5 — A properly modulated signal at A. The results of overmodulation are visible at B. This distorted signal creates spurious emissions which cause interference on nearby frequencies.**

**G8A09** **What type of modulation is used by the FT8 digital mode?**

A. 8-tone frequency shift keying
B. Vestigial sideband
C. Amplitude compressed AM
D. Direct sequence spread spectrum

**(A)** Both FT8 and JT65 use precisely timed sequences of transmit and receive, 8-tone FSK modulation, and sophisticated error decoding and correction techniques to enable successful decoding at very low signal-to-noise ratios (SNR). [*General Class License Manual*, page 6-9]

**G8A10** **What is meant by the term "flat-topping," when referring to a single sideband phone transmission?**

A. Signal distortion caused by insufficient collector current
B. The transmitter's automatic level control (ALC) is properly adjusted
C. Signal distortion caused by excessive drive
D. The transmitter's carrier is properly suppressed

**(C)** **Figure G8.6** shows an overmodulated signal as seen on an oscilloscope with flattening at the maximum levels of the envelope. This is referred to as flat-topping. [*General Class License Manual*, page 5-10]

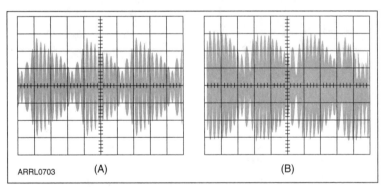

ARRL0703    (A)                                    (B)

**Figure G8.6 — Part A shows the output of a properly adjusted SSB transmitter. Part B shows the effects of overmodulation causing the highest peaks of the waveform to be limited or clipped, often referred to as flat-topping due to the flattening of the waveform envelope at a maximum value.**

**G8A11   What is the modulation envelope of an AM signal?**

    A. The waveform created by connecting the peak values of the modulated signal

    B. The carrier frequency that contains the signal

    C. Spurious signals that envelop nearby frequencies

    D. The bandwidth of the modulated signal

**(A)**    See question G8A05 and **Figure G8.4** for an illustration of an AM waveform's modulation envelope. [*General Class License Manual*, page 5-10]


**G8A12   Which of the following narrow-band digital modes can receive signals with very low signal-to-noise ratios?**

    A. MSK144

    B. FT8

    C. AMTOR

    D. MFSK32

**(B)**    See G8A09. [*General Class License Manual*, page 6-9]


## G8B — Frequency mixing; multiplication; bandwidths of various modes; deviation; duty cycle; intermodulation

**G8B01   Which mixer input is varied or tuned to convert signals of different frequencies to an intermediate frequency (IF)?**

    A. Image frequency

    B. Local oscillator

    C. RF input

    D. Beat frequency oscillator

**(B)**    The local oscillator (LO) is adjusted so that the desired signal creates a mixing product at a fixed frequency, called the intermediate frequency (IF). [*General Class License Manual*, page 5-16]

**G8B02** **If a receiver mixes a 13.800 MHz VFO with a 14.255 MHz received signal to produce a 455 kHz intermediate frequency (IF) signal, what type of interference will a 13.345 MHz signal produce in the receiver?**

A. Quadrature noise
B. Image response
C. Mixer interference
D. Intermediate interference

**(B)**    A mixer combines signals from an RF input and a local oscillator (LO) to produce mixing product signals with frequencies that are the sum and difference of the RF and LO signals (**Figure G8.7**). In a superheterodyne receiver, one of the new signals at the intermediate frequency (IF) is further amplified and demodulated. For example, if a 13.795 MHz LO signal is mixed with a 14.25 MHz RF signal, it will result in mixing products at 28.045 MHz and 0.455 MHz, or 455 kHz. A filter then removes the 28.045 MHz signal and passes the 455 kHz signal to the IF amplifier stages. In this case the input signal is 14.255 MHz and the oscillator signal is 13.800 MHz. The mixing products from these two signals are at 28.055 MHz and 0.455 MHz or 455 kHz, which is the intermediate frequency or IF. A signal at 13.455 MHz, when subtracted from the 13.800 MHz oscillator signal will also produce the 455 kHz intermediate frequency. When an undesired input signal also produces a signal at the intermediate frequency, the resulting interference is called image response interference. One way to reduce image response interference is to use an input filter to block signals outside of the desired range. [*General Class License Manual*, page 5-18]

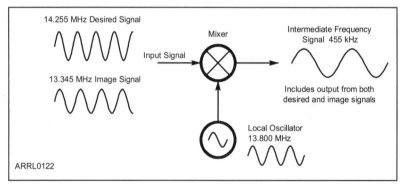

**Figure G8.7 — A mixer stage combines an RF input signal with a local oscillator (LO) signal to produce mixing products with frequencies of the sum and difference of the RF and LO frequencies. In a receiver, one of the mixing products at the intermediate frequency (IF) signal is further amplified and demodulated. An undesired signal at the image frequency can also produce a mixing product at the IF, interfering with the desired RF signal.**

**G8B03    What is another term for the mixing of two RF signals?**

A. Heterodyning
B. Synthesizing
C. Cancellation
D. Phase inverting

**(A)**    The process of mixing signals is known as heterodyning. A receiver that mixes a local oscillator (LO) signal with a received RF signal to produce a signal at some intermediate frequency (IF) that is higher in frequency than the baseband audio signal is called a superheterodyne or superhet receiver. The IF signal is processed further by filtering and amplifying it, and then converting the signal to baseband audio. The audio signal is further amplified and fed to a speaker or is connected to headphones so you can hear the received signal. [*General Class License Manual*, page 5-5]

**G8B04    What is the stage in a VHF FM transmitter that generates a harmonic of a lower frequency signal to reach the desired operating frequency?**

A. Mixer
B. Reactance modulator
C. Pre-emphasis network
D. Multiplier

**(D)**    In a VHF FM transmitter, a reactance modulator operates on a radio-frequency oscillator that is normally operating in the high frequency (HF) range. A frequency multiplier doubles or triples the frequency of the modulated signal, usually by generating harmonics of the modulated HF signal and selecting one for output to the next stage in the transmitter. Sometimes several multiplier stages are required to produce a signal at the desired output frequency. [*General Class License Manual*, page 5-5]

**G8B05    What is the approximate bandwidth of a PACTOR-III signal at maximum data rate?**

A. 31.5 Hz
B. 500 Hz
C. 1800 Hz
D. 2300 Hz

**(D)**    PACTOR is a digital mode that has several versions from the original PACTOR 1 through the current PACTOR 4 or PACTOR IV. The PACTOR 3 protocol has the ability to vary its symbol rate in response to conditions between the two stations making contact. As symbol rate increases, so does the required signal bandwidth. At the maximum symbol rate, PACTOR 3 signals occupy approximately 2300 Hz. [*General Class License Manual*, page 6-10]

**G8B06**  **What is the total bandwidth of an FM phone transmission having 5 kHz deviation and 3 kHz modulating frequency?**

    A.  3 kHz
    B.  5 kHz
    C.  8 kHz
    D.  16 kHz

**(D)**    To determine bandwidth of an FM-phone transmission, use the following formula, called Carson's Rule:

$$BW = 2 \times (D + M)$$

where:

BW = bandwidth

D = frequency deviation (the instantaneous change in frequency for a given signal)

M = maximum modulating audio frequency

The total bandwidth of an FM phone transmission having a 5 kHz deviation and a 3 kHz modulating frequency would be:

$$2 \times (5 \text{ kHz} + 3 \text{ kHz}) = 16 \text{ kHz}$$

[*General Class License Manual*, page 5-10]


**G8B07**  **What is the frequency deviation for a 12.21 MHz reactance modulated oscillator in a 5 kHz deviation, 146.52 MHz FM phone transmitter?**

    A.  101.75 Hz
    B.  416.7 Hz
    C.  5 kHz
    D.  60 kHz

**(B)**    See G8B04. When an FM signal's frequency is multiplied, the deviation is also multiplied. This is why the deviation of the modulated oscillator is less than that of the final output signal. To determine the required oscillator frequency deviation, divide the transmitter's output frequency by the oscillator frequency to determine the multiplication factor of the transmitter:

$$\text{Multiplication factor} = \frac{\text{Transmitter output frequency}}{\text{Oscillator frequency}}$$

The multiplication factor for this transmitter is 146.52 MHz / 12.21 MHz = 12. Next divide the desired output deviation by the multiplication factor to obtain the deviation required in the oscillator: 5 kHz / 12 = 416.7 Hz. [*General Class License Manual*, page 5-10]

**G8B08** **Why is it important to know the duty cycle of the mode you are using when transmitting?**

A. To aid in tuning your transmitter
B. Some modes have high duty cycles that could exceed the transmitter's average power rating
C. To allow time for the other station to break in during a transmission
D. The attenuator will have to be adjusted accordingly

**(B)** Most Amateur Radio transmitters are not designed to operate at full power output for an extended time. The final output stage is not able to dissipate all of the excess heat generated when the transmitter is continuously producing full output power. When you are operating CW, for example, the transmitter is turned on and off to form the Morse code characters so that the transmitter is only operating at full power about 40 to 50% of the time. During the off times, the amplifier stage cools sufficiently to allow full-power operation. When you are operating single-sideband voice, the transmitter is producing full power only when your voice reaches maximum amplitude. For a typical SSB conversation, the transmitter is operating at full power only about 20 to 25% of the time.

When you are operating some digital modes, however, your transmitter may be operating at full power the entire time you are transmitting. For radioteletype the transmitter is producing full output power, switching between the mark and space tones, so the duty cycle is 100%. For PSK31 and similar modes, the transmitter is producing full power for virtually the entire transmit time, so the duty cycle is 100%. PACTOR, packet radio and a few other modes have slightly reduced duty cycles because the transmitter sends some data and then waits to receive an acknowledgement. If you are operating a high-duty-cycle mode you should reduce your transmit power to prevent overheating the amplifier. Consult your radio's manual to determine the manufacturer's recommendations or reduce power output to 50% or less of full power when operating using a digital mode. [*General Class License Manual*, page 6-10]

**G8B09** **Why is it good to match receiver bandwidth to the bandwidth of the operating mode?**

A. It is required by FCC rules
B. It minimizes power consumption in the receiver
C. It improves impedance matching of the antenna
D. It results in the best signal-to-noise ratio

**(D)** By matching the receiver bandwidth and the signal bandwidth, noise outside the signal's bandwidth is rejected and no necessary signal energy is discarded. Both result in improvement of the received signal-to-noise ratio (SNR). [*General Class License Manual*, page 5-18]

### G8B10 What is the relationship between transmitted symbol rate and bandwidth?

A. Symbol rate and bandwidth are not related
B. Higher symbol rates require wider bandwidth
C. Lower symbol rates require wider bandwidth
D. Bandwidth is always half the symbol rate

**(B)** Advanced modulation techniques can pack multiple bits of data into each transmitted symbol, but it is the symbol rate that sets a minimum limit on bandwidth. Increasing the rate at which symbols are transmitted requires more signal bandwidth in order to maintain a minimum signal-to-noise ratio. [*General Class License Manual*, page 6-10]

### G8B11 What combination of a mixer's Local Oscillator (LO) and RF input frequencies is found in the output?

A. The ratio
B. The average
C. The sum and difference
D. The arithmetic product

**(C)** See G8B03. [*General Class License Manual*, page 5-5]

### G8B12 What process combines two signals in a non-linear circuit or connection to produce unwanted spurious outputs?

A. Intermodulation
B. Heterodyning
C. Detection
D. Rolloff

**(A)** Nonlinear connections or circuits can act as a mixer and generate mixing products from any signals that are present. [*General Class License Manual*, page 5-24]

## G8C — Digital emission modes

### G8C01 On what band do amateurs share channels with the unlicensed Wi-Fi service?

A. 432 MHz
B. 902 MHz
C. 2.4 GHz
D. 10.7 GHz

**(C)** Hams share some spectrum in the 13-centimeter (2.3 GHz) band with Wi-Fi channels and may even use some of the Wi-Fi protocols but amateurs may not communicate with unlicensed Wi-Fi stations. [*General Class License Manual*, page 3-8]

**G8C02** **Which digital mode is used as a low-power beacon for assessing HF propagation?**

A. WSPR
B. Olivia
C. PSK31
D. SSB-SC

**(A)** WSPR (Whisper) is designed to experiment with and assess HF propagation paths at very low signal-to-noise ratios. WSPR does not support two-way QSOs and acts as a very narrow bandwidth beacon. [*General Class License Manual*, page 6-9]

**G8C03** **What part of a packet radio frame contains the routing and handling information?**

A. Directory
B. Preamble
C. Header
D. Footer

**(C)** Packet radio and other packetized protocols combine the message to be transferred with control and routing instructions in groups called frames. Each frame is transmitted separately. The entire message is then reassembled at the destination from the received frames. Frames begin with a header that contains information about the routing and handling of the frame. Headers are followed by the data section of the frame and a short terminating segment called the trailer that tells the receiver the frame is complete. Error detection and correction information can also be included in the header or trailer, depending on the protocol being used. [*General Class License Manual*, page 6-7]

**G8C04** **Which of the following describes Baudot code?**

A. A 7-bit code with start, stop, and parity bits
B. A code using error detection and correction
C. A 5-bit code with additional start and stop bits
D. A code using SELCAL and LISTEN

**(C)** The Baudot code used for radioteletype (RTTY) has five data bits per character. This limits the code to $2^5 = 32$ possible characters but special characters (LTRS and FIGS) switch the code between two character sets: capital letters or numbers and punctuation. So the receiver can decode the characters from the transmitted signal, an additional START and STOP bit are transmitted with each character. [*General Class License Manual*, page 6-5]

**G8C05** **In the PACTOR protocol, what is meant by a NAK response to a transmitted packet?**

A. The receiver is requesting the packet be retransmitted
B. The receiver is reporting the packet was received without error
C. The receiver is busy decoding the packet
D. The entire file has been received correctly

**(A)** PACTOR is an ARQ mode, meaning "Automatic Repeat reQuest", in which errors in received data generate a NAK response transmission by the receiving station, causing the transmitting station to send the frame again. If the frame is received correctly, an ACK response transmission is made so the transmitter can send the next frame. [*General Class License Manual*, page 6-7]

**G8C06** **What action results from a failure to exchange information due to excessive transmission attempts when using PACTOR or WINMOR?**

A. The checksum overflows
B. The connection is dropped
C. Packets will be routed incorrectly
D. Encoding reverts to the default character set

**(B)** Sometimes conditions are unable to sustain an error-free exchange of data, resulting in repeated NAK responses (see G8C05) that would never stop. To prevent occupying a channel when communications is not possible, either station may decide to terminate the connection between stations when too many NAK responses have been received or transmitted. Connections can also "time out" and be terminated when no frame has been received or the receiver has not responded for a specified time. [*General Class License Manual*, page 6-14]

**G8C07** **How does the receiving station respond to an ARQ data mode packet containing errors?**

A. It terminates the contact
B. It requests the packet be retransmitted
C. It sends the packet back to the transmitting station
D. It requests a change in transmitting protocol

**(B)** ARQ stands for Automatic Repeat request. In a mode using ARQ, if a transmitted frame is received with errors, the receiving station will transmit a NAK response that notifies the transmitter to send the frame again. An ACK response indicates that the frame was received correctly. [*General Class License Manual*, page 6-7]

**G8C08    Which of the following statements is true about PSK31?**

A. Upper case letters are sent with more power
B. Upper case letters use longer Varicode bit sequences and thus slow down transmission
C. Error correction is used to ensure accurate message reception
D. Higher power is needed as compared to RTTY for similar error rates

**(B)**    In Varicode, the encoding scheme used by PSK31, the most common characters are sent using shorter codes to speed up transmissions. Upper-case letters are less common than lower-case and were assigned longer codes. Thus, unlike RTTY which uses only upper-case letters, capital letters take longer to transmit than lower-case in PSK31. [*General Class License Manual*, page 6-6]

**G8C09    What does the number 31 represent in "PSK31"?**

A. The approximate transmitted symbol rate
B. The version of the PSK protocol
C. The year in which PSK31 was invented
D. The number of characters that can be represented by PSK31

**(A)**    PSK31 is a digital mode that transmits symbols at a rate of 31.25 baud. [*General Class License Manual*, page 6-5]

**G8C10    How does forward error correction (FEC) allow the receiver to correct errors in received data packets?**

A. By controlling transmitter output power for optimum signal strength
B. By using the Varicode character set
C. By transmitting redundant information with the data
D. By using a parity bit with each character

**(C)**    Forward error correction (FEC) is the practice of sending redundant data in the transmitted frame that allows the receiver to correct some types of errors that may be caused by noise, fading or interference. There are a number of FEC methods involving special codes. [*General Class License Manual*, page 6-7]

**G8C11    How are the two separate frequencies of a Frequency Shift Keyed (FSK) signal identified?**

A. Dot and dash
B. On and off
C. High and low
D. Mark and space

**(D)**    For an FSK signal that uses two tones (MFSK or multiple-FSK modulation uses more than two tones), a Mark tone represents a digital bit value of 1 and a Space tone represents a 0. [*General Class License Manual*, page 6-4]

**G8C12** **Which type of code is used for sending characters in a PSK31 signal?**

A. Varicode
B. Viterbi
C. Volumetric
D. Binary

**(A)** Unlike most other digital modes which use fixed-length codes for each transmitted symbol, PSK31 uses a variable-length code called Varicode in which the more common characters use shorter codes to save transmission time, just as Morse code does. [*General Class License Manual*, page 6-5]

**G8C13** **What is indicated on a waterfall display by one or more vertical lines on either side of a digital signal?**

A. Long path propagation
B. Backscatter propagation
C. Insufficient modulation
D. Overmodulation

**(D)** On a waterfall display like that of **Figure G8.8**, strong signals sometimes seem to have nearby "ghosts" that follow them down the screen, usually as one to three parallel lines. These are distortion products caused by overdriving the transceiver microphone input with the AFSK signals or by the ALC system distorting the RF signal as it changes transmitter power levels. You can get rid of these unwanted spurious emissions by reducing audio levels and setting power levels so that the ALC system is not activated. [*General Class License Manual*, page 6-11]

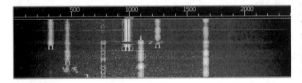

**Figure G8.8 — A waterfall display shows signal strength and frequency as a series of lines moving down the display.**

**G8C14** **Which of the following describes a waterfall display?**

A. Frequency is horizontal, signal strength is vertical, time is intensity
B. Frequency is vertical, signal strength is intensity, time is horizontal
C. Frequency is horizontal, signal strength is intensity, time is vertical
D. Frequency is vertical, signal strength is horizontal, time is intensity

**(C)** A waterfall display is composed of lines which show signal strength across a band of frequencies as intensity or color. As each new scan is displayed, the older lines move down, giving the impression of a waterfall. The most common waterfall display shows frequency horizontally although a few programs have the option of setting the display to "move" horizontally. [*General Class License Manual*, page 6-13]

# Antennas and Feed Lines

Your General class exam (Element 3) will consist of 35 questions taken from the General class question pool as prepared by the Volunteer Examiner Coordinators' Question Pool Committee. A certain number of questions are taken from each of the 10 subelements. There will be 4 questions from the subelement shown in this chapter. These questions are divided into 4 groups, labeled G9A through G9D.

## SUBELEMENT G9 — ANTENNAS AND FEED LINES
### [4 Exam Questions — 4 Groups]

### G9A — Antenna feed lines: characteristic impedance and attenuation; SWR calculation, measurement, and effects; matching networks

**G9A01**    Which of the following factors determine the characteristic impedance of a parallel conductor antenna feed line?

A. The distance between the centers of the conductors and the radius of the conductors

B. The distance between the centers of the conductors and the length of the line

C. The radius of the conductors and the frequency of the signal

D. The frequency of the signal and the length of the line

**(A)**    The characteristic impedance of a parallel-conductor feed line (**Figure G9.1**) depends on the distance between the conductor centers and the radius of the conductors. [*General Class License Manual*, page 7-21]

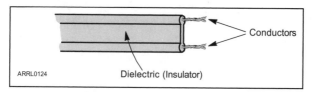

**Figure G9.1 —The construction of common 300-ohm twin lead — one form of parallel-conductor feed line.**

**G9A02** What are the typical characteristic impedances of coaxial cables used for antenna feed lines at amateur stations?

A. 25 and 30 ohms
B. 50 and 75 ohms
C. 80 and 100 ohms
D. 500 and 750 ohms

**(B)** Common coaxial cables (**Figure G9.2** ) used as antenna feed lines have characteristic impedances of 50 or 75 ohms. See. [*General Class License Manual*, page 7-21]

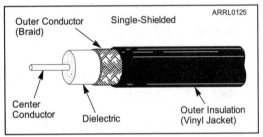

**Figure G9.2 — Coaxial cables consist of a conductor surrounded by an insulating dielectric. A second conductor, called the shield, surrounds the insulation. A plastic jacket then covers the entire cable.**

**G9A03** What is the typical characteristic impedance of "window line" parallel transmission line?

A. 50 ohms
B. 75 ohms
C. 100 ohms
D. 450 ohms

**(D)** The most common type of parallel-conductor line is window line that has solid plastic insulation between the conductors with rectangular "windows" cut out of the insulation to reduce loss and weight. The typical impedance for window line is 450 Ω although there are several variations as low as 400 Ω. [*General Class License Manual*, page 7-21]

**G9A04**    **What might cause reflected power at the point where a feed line connects to an antenna?**

A. Operating an antenna at its resonant frequency
B. Using more transmitter power than the antenna can handle
C. A difference between feed-line impedance and antenna feed-point impedance
D. Feeding the antenna with unbalanced feed line

**(C)**    Whenever power traveling along a feed line encounters a different impedance from the characteristic impedance of the feed line, such as at an antenna, some of the power is reflected back toward the power source. The greater the difference between the feed line's characteristic impedance and the new impedance, the larger the fraction of power that is reflected. [*General Class License Manual*, page 7-21]

**G9A05**    **How does the attenuation of coaxial cable change as the frequency of the signal it is carrying increases?**

A. Attenuation is independent of frequency
B. Attenuation increases
C. Attenuation decreases
D. Attenuation reaches a maximum at approximately 18 MHz

**(B)**    Feed line loss is greater at higher frequencies. For example, if you were to use the same type of coaxial cable for your 160 meter antenna as for your 2 meter antenna, there would be much more loss at the higher 2 meter frequencies. [*General Class License Manual*, page 7-23]

**G9A06**    **In what units is RF feed line loss usually expressed?**

A. Ohms per 1000 feet
B. Decibels per 1000 feet
C. Ohms per 100 feet
D. Decibels per 100 feet

**(D)**    RF feed line loss is normally specified in decibels of loss for 100 feet of line. Because it changes with frequency, loss is also specified at a certain frequency [*General Class License Manual*, page 7-23]

**G9A07** **What must be done to prevent standing waves on an antenna feed line?**

A. The antenna feed point must be at DC ground potential
B. The feed line must be cut to a length equal to an odd number of electrical quarter wavelengths
C. The feed line must be cut to a length equal to an even number of physical half wavelengths
D. The antenna feed point impedance must be matched to the characteristic impedance of the feed line

**(D)** To eliminate reflected power, the antenna impedance must be matched to the characteristic impedance of the feed line. If the impedances are matched, all of the feed line power is transferred to the antenna. [*General Class License Manual*, page 7-22]

**G9A08** **If the SWR on an antenna feed line is 5 to 1, and a matching network at the transmitter end of the feed line is adjusted to 1 to 1 SWR, what is the resulting SWR on the feed line?**

A. 1 to 1
B. 5 to 1
C. Between 1 to 1 and 5 to 1 depending on the characteristic impedance of the line
D. Between 1 to 1 and 5 to 1 depending on the reflected power at the transmitter

**(B)** A matching network at the transmitter does not change the SWR on the feed line, so the feed line SWR is still 5:1. [*General Class License Manual*, page 7-22]

**G9A09** **What standing wave ratio will result when connecting a 50 ohm feed line to a non-reactive load having 200 ohm impedance?**

A. 4:1
B. 1:4
C. 2:1
D. 1:2

**(A)** If a load connected to a feed line is purely resistive, the SWR can be calculated by dividing the line characteristic impedance by the load resistance or vice versa, whichever gives a value greater than one. 200 / 50 = 4:1 SWR. [*General Class License Manual*, page 7-21]

**G9A10**   **What standing wave ratio will result when connecting a 50 ohm feed line to a non-reactive load having 10 ohm impedance?**

    A.  2:1
    B.  50:1
    C.  1:5
    D.  5:1

**(D)**    If a load connected to a feed line is purely resistive, the SWR can be calculated by dividing the line characteristic impedance by the load resistance or vice versa, whichever gives a value greater than one. 50 / 10 = 5:1 SWR. [*General Class License Manual*, page 7-21]

**G9A11**   **What standing wave ratio will result when connecting a 50 ohm feed line to a non-reactive load having 50 ohm impedance?**

    A.  2:1
    B.  1:1
    C.  50:50
    D.  0:0

**(B)**    If a load connected to a feed line is purely resistive, the SWR can be calculated by dividing the line characteristic impedance by the load resistance or vice versa, whichever gives a value greater than one. 50 / 50 = 1:1 SWR. [*General Class License Manual*, page 7-21]

**G9A12**   **What is the interaction between high standing wave ratio (SWR) and transmission line loss?**

    A.  There is no interaction between transmission line loss and SWR
    B.  If a transmission line is lossy, high SWR will increase the loss
    C.  High SWR makes it difficult to measure transmission line loss
    D.  High SWR reduces the relative effect of transmission line loss

**(B)**    Power reflected back from an antenna or load because the SWR is greater than 1:1 returns to the source of the power, such as a transmitter. The transmitter in turn reflects the power back toward the antenna, creating a standing wave. When the feed line and antenna impedances are not matched, less power is transferred to the antenna because of the extra loss incurred as the reflected power travels up and down the feed line. The higher the SWR, the more power is reflected and thus lost. [*General Class License Manual*, page 7-23]

### G9A13    What is the effect of transmission line loss on SWR measured at the input to the line?

A. The higher the transmission line loss, the more the SWR will read artificially low
B. The higher the transmission line loss, the more the SWR will read artificially high
C. The higher the transmission line loss, the more accurate the SWR measurement will be
D. Transmission line loss does not affect the SWR measurement

**(A)**    SWR is almost always measured at the transmitter end of an antenna feed line. The SWR is calculated by measuring the forward power (PF) and reflected power (PR). (See question G4B10 for the exact formula.) If power reflected from the antenna is lost in the feed line before it reaches the measurement point at the transmitter end, it will appear that less was reflected from the antenna, reducing the measured value of SWR. [*General Class License Manual*, page 7-23]

## G9B — Basic antennas

### G9B01    What is one disadvantage of a directly fed random-wire HF antenna?

A. It must be longer than 1 wavelength
B. You may experience RF burns when touching metal objects in your station
C. It produces only vertically polarized radiation
D. It is more effective on the lower HF bands than on the higher bands

**(B)**    A random-wire antenna is connected directly to the transmitter at one end. It can be of any length because an antenna tuner is used to match the impedance of the antenna. There is no feed line. One significant disadvantage of a random-wire antenna is that you may experience RF "hot spots" in your station because the station equipment and wiring are part of your antenna system! [*General Class License Manual*, page 7-16]

**G9B02** Which of the following is a common way to adjust the feed-point impedance of a quarter wave ground-plane vertical antenna to be approximately 50 ohms?

A. Slope the radials upward
B. Slope the radials downward
C. Lengthen the radials
D. Shorten the radials

**(B)** A ground-plane antenna is often constructed with a ¼-wavelength vertical radiating element and four ¼-wavelength horizontal "radial" wires that form the ground plane. You can change the impedance of a ground-plane antenna by changing the angle of the radials. Bending or sloping the radials downward to about a 45-degree angle will increase the impedance from approximately 35 ohms to approximately 50 ohms which is a better match to most coaxial feed lines. See **Figure G9.3**. [*General Class License Manual*, page 7-5]

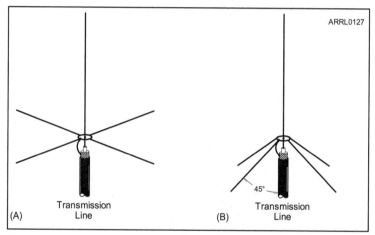

Figure G9.3 — A ground-plane antenna may use horizontal (A) or downward-sloping radials. By sloping the radials down (B), the feed point impedance is raised closer to 50 ohms, presenting a better impedance match to 50-ohm coaxial cable.

**G9B03** Which of the following best describes the radiation pattern of a quarter-wave, ground-plane vertical antenna?

A. Bi-directional in azimuth
B. Isotropic
C. Hemispherical
D. Omnidirectional in azimuth

**(D)** Ground-planes are often called "verticals" because that is the usual way of constructing and installing them. Like a dipole, the ground-plane radiates best broadside to its axis. If installed vertically, this means the ground-plane antenna's pattern is omnidirectional, uniform in all azimuth angles or directions. [*General Class License Manual*, page 7-4]

**G9B04**   **What is the radiation pattern of a dipole antenna in free space in a plane containing the conductor?**

A. It is a figure-eight at right angles to the antenna
B. It is a figure-eight off both ends of the antenna
C. It is a circle (equal radiation in all directions)
D. It has a pair of lobes on one side of the antenna and a single lobe on the other side

**(A)**    A ½-wavelength dipole antenna radiates its signals in a bi-directional fashion with maximum radiation at right-angles to the antenna, as shown in **Figure G9.4**. This is called a "figure 8" radiation pattern. [*General Class License Manual*, page 7-2]

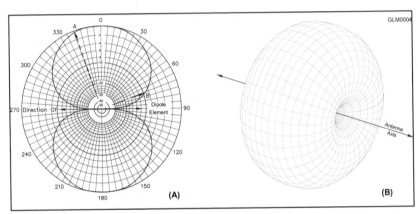

Figure G9.4 — Part A shows the radiation pattern in the plane of a dipole located in free space. The dipole element is located on the line from 270 to 90 degrees in this figure. Part B shows the three-dimensional radiation pattern in all directions around the dipole.

**G9B05**   **How does antenna height affect the horizontal (azimuthal) radiation pattern of a horizontal dipole HF antenna?**

A. If the antenna is too high, the pattern becomes unpredictable
B. Antenna height has no effect on the pattern
C. If the antenna is less than ½ wavelength high, the azimuthal pattern is almost omnidirectional
D. If the antenna is less than ½ wavelength high, radiation off the ends of the wire is eliminated

**(C)**    As height is reduced below ½-wavelength the antenna pattern of the dipole becomes almost omnidirectional because of reflections from the ground. This antenna transmits and receives nearly equally in all compass directions although at a high vertical angle. [*General Class License Manual*, page 7-6]

**G9B06** **Where should the radial wires of a ground-mounted vertical antenna system be placed?**

A. As high as possible above the ground
B. Parallel to the antenna element
C. On the surface of the Earth or buried a few inches below the ground
D. At the center of the antenna

**(C)** In most installations, the soil is too lossy to act as an effective ground plane, so an artificial ground screen must be made from radial wires placed on the ground near the base of the antenna. These radials are usually ¼ wavelength or longer (they are not resonant). Depending on ground conductivity, 8, 16, 32 or more radials may be required to form an effective ground. The radial wires of a ground-mounted vertical antenna should be placed on the Earth's surface or buried a few inches below the surface. [*General Class License Manual*, page 7-4]

**G9B07** **How does the feed point impedance of a ½ wave dipole antenna change as the antenna is lowered below ¼ wave above ground?**

A. It steadily increases
B. It steadily decreases
C. It peaks at about ⅛ wavelength above ground
D. It is unaffected by the height above ground

**(B)** As the antenna is lowered below ¼ wavelength above ground, the impedance steadily decreases to a very low value when placed directly on the ground. [*General Class License Manual*, page 7-6]

**G9B08** **How does the feed point impedance of a ½ wave dipole change as the feed point is moved from the center toward the ends?**

A. It steadily increases
B. It steadily decreases
C. It peaks at about ⅛ wavelength from the end
D. It is unaffected by the location of the feed point

**(A)** The center of a ½-wavelength dipole is the location of the lowest feed point impedance, approximately 72 ohms in free space. At the ends of the dipole, feed point impedance is several thousand ohms. In between, feed point impedance increases steadily as the feed point is moved from the center toward the ends of the antenna. [*General Class License Manual*, page 7-3]

**G9B09** **Which of the following is an advantage of a horizontally polarized as compared to a vertically polarized HF antenna?**

A. Lower ground reflection losses
B. Lower feed-point impedance
C. Shorter radials
D. Lower radiation resistance

**(A)** The signals from a horizontally polarized antenna have lower losses when reflecting from the ground. This is because the horizontal polarization of the wave induces currents that flow along the surface of the ground. Vertical polarization tends to induce currents that flow vertically in the ground, where losses are higher.

Radio waves reflecting from the ground have lower losses when the polarization of the wave is parallel to the ground. That is, when the waves are horizontally polarized. Because the reflected waves combine with the direct waves (not reflected) to make up the antenna's radiation pattern, lower reflection loss results in stronger signal strength.

Ground-mounted vertical antennas, however, are able to generate stronger signals at low angles of radiation than horizontally polarized antennas at low heights. This means they are often preferred for DX contacts on the lower HF bands where it is impractical to raise horizontally polarized antennas to the height necessary for strong low-angle signals. [*General Class License Manual*, page 7-7]

**G9B10**  What is the approximate length for a ½ wave dipole antenna cut for 14.250 MHz?

A. 8 feet
B. 16 feet
C. 24 feet
D. 33 feet

**(D)**    In free space, ½ wavelength in feet equals 492 divided by frequency in MHz. If you cut a piece of wire that length, however, you'll find it is too long to resonate at the desired frequency. A resonant ½-wave dipole made of ordinary wire will be shorter than the free-space wavelength for several reasons. First, the physical thickness of the wire makes it look a bit longer electrically than it is physically. The thicker the wire or the lower its length-to-diameter (l/d) ratio, the shorter it will be when it is resonant. Second, the dipole's height above ground also affects its resonant frequency. In addition, nearby conductors, insulation on the wire, the means by which the wire is secured to the insulators and to the feed line also affect the resonant length. For these reasons, a single universal formula for dipole length, such as the common 468/f, is not very useful. You should start with a length near the free-space length and be prepared to trim the dipole to resonance using an SWR meter or antenna analyzer. The exam only requires that you identify an approximate resonant length for a dipole. Use the free-space length, calculated as 492 / f (in MHz), and select the closest choice. In this case, length (feet) = 492 / 14.250 = 34.5 feet, so select the closest value — 33 feet. [*General Class License Manual*, page 7-4]

**G9B11**  What is the approximate length for a ½ wave dipole antenna cut for 3.550 MHz?

A. 42 feet
B. 84 feet
C. 132 feet
D. 263 feet

**(C)**    (See also G9B10.) Calculate length (feet) = 492 / 3.550 = 139 ft. The closest value is 132 feet. [*General Class License Manual*, page 7-3]

**G9B12**  What is the approximate length for a ¼ wave vertical antenna cut for 28.5 MHz?

A. 8 feet
B. 11 feet
C. 16 feet
D. 21 feet

**(A)**    (See also G9B10.) A ¼-wavelength antenna would be half as long as a ½-wavelength antenna so calculate length (feet) = 246 / 28.5 = 8.6 ft. The closest value is 8 feet. [*General Class License Manual*, page 7-5]

## G9C — Directional antennas

**G9C01**  Which of the following would increase the bandwidth of a Yagi antenna?

A. Larger-diameter elements
B. Closer element spacing
C. Loading coils in series with the element
D. Tapered-diameter elements

**(A)**  Using larger diameter elements increases the SWR bandwidth of a parasitic beam antenna, such as a Yagi antenna as shown in **Figure G9.5**. The exact length of the elements becomes less critical when larger diameter elements are used. [*General Class License Manual*, page 7-10]

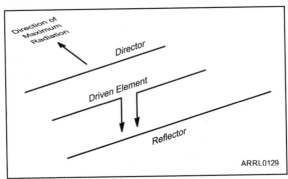

**Figure G9.5 — A typical three-element Yagi antenna showing the relative lengths of the elements and the direction of the antenna's main lobe.**

**G9C02**  What is the approximate length of the driven element of a Yagi antenna?

A. ¼ wavelength
B. ½ wavelength
C. ¾ wavelength
D. 1 wavelength

**(B)**  A Yagi antenna consists of a driven element that is close to ½-wavelength long with one or more parasitic elements that help direct the radiated energy in one direction. Directors are parasitic elements that are mounted along the antenna's supporting boom in the preferred direction of radiation and reflectors are mounted in the opposite direction. [*General Class License Manual*, page 7-10]

**G9C03** **How do the lengths of a three-element Yagi reflector and director compare to that of the driven element?**

A. The reflector is longer, and the director is shorter
B. The reflector is shorter, and the director is longer
C. They are all the same length
D. Relative length depends on the frequency of operation

**(A)** A Yagi's elements are physically arranged to create gain in a single major or main lobe and cancel signals in the opposite direction. The parasitic elements placed in the direction of maximum gain are called directors and are slightly shorter than the driven element. Parasitic elements in the direction of minimum gain are called reflectors and are slightly longer than the driven element. [*General Class License Manual*, page 7-10]

**G9C04** **How does antenna gain stated in dBi compare to gain stated in dBd for the same antenna?**

A. dBi gain figures are 2.15 dB lower than dBd gain figures
B. dBi gain figures are 2.15 dB higher than dBd gain figures
C. dBi gain figures are the same as the square root of dBd gain figures multiplied by 2.15
D. dBi gain figures are the reciprocal of dBd gain figures + 2.15 dB

**(B)** (See G9C15.) The gain of the reference dipole with respect to the isotropic antenna is 2.15 dB. To convert gain from dBd to dBi, add 2.15 dB. [*General Class License Manual*, page 7-3]

**G9C05** **How does increasing boom length and adding directors affect a Yagi antenna?**

A. Gain increases
B. Beamwidth increases
C. Front-to-back ratio decreases
D. Front-to-side ratio decreases

**(A)** As the boom length of a Yagi is increased and more elements are added, the directivity or gain of the antenna increases. Directivity has an advantage in that it concentrates the transmitted and received signals in the intended direction more than in other directions, thus minimizing interference and improving the signal-to-noise ratio of received signals. [*General Class License Manual*, page 7-10]

**G9C06** **What configuration of the loops of a two-element quad antenna must be used for the antenna to operate as a beam antenna, assuming one of the elements is used as a reflector?**

A. The driven element must be fed with a balun transformer
B. There must be an open circuit in the driven element at the point opposite the feed point
C. The reflector element must be approximately 5 percent shorter than the driven element
D. The reflector element must be approximately 5 percent longer than the driven element

**(D)** The common quad antenna with square elements operates identically to a conventional Yagi using straight elements. (See also G9C03.) [*General Class License Manual*, page 7-13]

**G9C07** **What does "front-to-back ratio" mean in reference to a Yagi antenna?**

A. The number of directors versus the number of reflectors
B. The relative position of the driven element with respect to the reflectors and directors
C. The power radiated in the major radiation lobe compared to that in the opposite direction
D. The ratio of forward gain to dipole gain

**(C)** Using a directional antenna helps reduce interference in that it sends and receives better in the intended direction rather than off to the side or rear. Most of the radiated signal is sent in the desired direction. If you measure the power radiated in the desired direction and compare it with the power radiated in the exactly opposite direction, that is the antenna's front-to-back ratio as shown in **Figure G9.6**. [*General Class License Manual*, page 7-10]

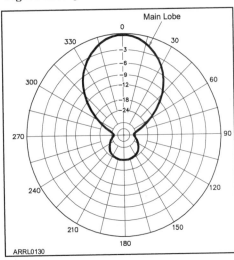

Figure G9.6 — The directive pattern for a typical three-element Yagi antenna. Note that this pattern is essentially unidirectional, with most of the radiation in the direction of the main lobe. There is also a small minor lobe at 180° from the direction of the main lobe, however. You can read the front-to-back-ratio on this type of graph by finding the strength of the minor lobe off the back of the antenna. For this antenna, the front-to-back-ratio is 24 dB because the maximum signal at 180° just touches the −24 dB circle. That means the signal off the back of the antenna is 24 dB less than the signal from the front or forward direction of the antenna.

**G9C08**    What is meant by the "main lobe" of a directive antenna?

A. The magnitude of the maximum vertical angle of radiation
B. The point of maximum current in a radiating antenna element
C. The maximum voltage standing wave point on a radiating element
D. The direction of maximum radiated field strength from the antenna

**(D)**    A Yagi antenna radiates most of the signal in one direction. The range of directions in which the Yagi radiates and receives most strongly is called the main lobe of the antenna's radiation pattern. [*General Class License Manual*, page 7-9]

**G9C09**    How does the gain of two three-element, horizontally polarized Yagi antennas spaced vertically ½ wavelength apart typically compare to the gain of a single three-element Yagi?

A. Approximately 1.5 dB higher
B. Approximately 3 dB higher
C. Approximately 6 dB higher
D. Approximately 9 dB higher

**(B)**    Called vertical stacking, placing antennas one above the other provides additional focusing of the antenna's radiation pattern, increasing overall gain of the antenna system. A stack of two such antennas doubles gain which is equivalent to a 3 dB increase. [*General Class License Manual*, page 7-17]

**G9C10**    Which of the following can be adjusted to optimize forward gain, front-to-back ratio, or SWR bandwidth of a Yagi antenna?

A. The physical length of the boom
B. The number of elements on the boom
C. The spacing of each element along the boom
D. All these choices are correct

**(D)**    All of these choices affect a Yagi antenna's forward gain, front-to-back ratio and SWR bandwidth. As you might imagine, adjusting an antenna design for the desired combination of these three important parameters can be a complicated procedure. Computer modeling programs greatly simplify this process. [*General Class License Manual*, page 7-11]

**G9C11**    Which HF antenna would be the best to use for minimizing interference?

A. A quarter-wave vertical antenna
B. An isotropic antenna
C. A directional antenna
D. An omnidirectional antenna

**(C)**    Directional antennas are used widely because they create gain as well as reject interference and noise from other than the desired direction. [*General Class License Manual*, page 7-8]

**G9C12** **Which of the following is an advantage of using a gamma match with a Yagi antenna?**

A. It does not require that the driven element be insulated from the boom
B. It does not require any inductors or capacitors
C. It is useful for matching multiband antennas
D. All these choices are correct

**(A)** One major advantage of the gamma match (**Figure G9.7A** and **B**) is that the driven element does not have to be insulated from the antenna's boom. This simplifies the construction and mounting of the driven element. [*General Class License Manual*, page 7-12]

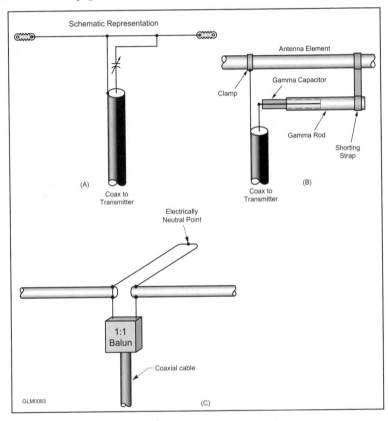

**Figure G9.7** — The gamma match (A and B) is a short section of transmission line that transforms a low impedance at the center of the driven element to a higher impedance closer to that of coaxial cable. The gamma match is tuned with the gamma capacitor and by moving the shorting strap. A is the schematic equivalent and B shows typical gamma match construction. C shows the beta or "hairpin" match. The beta match maintains driven element balance. The center point of the stub or hairpin is electrically neutral and can be connected directly to the antenna boom for mechanical stability.

### G9C13 Approximately how long is each side of the driven element of a quad antenna?

A. ¼ wavelength
B. ½ wavelength
C. ¾ wavelength
D. 1 wavelength

**(A)**   All of the elements of a quad antenna are square-shaped loops which are approximately a full wavelength in circumference, so each of the element's four sides is approximately ¼ wavelength long. **Figure G9.8** shows the quad's construction. [*General Class License Manual*, page 7-13]

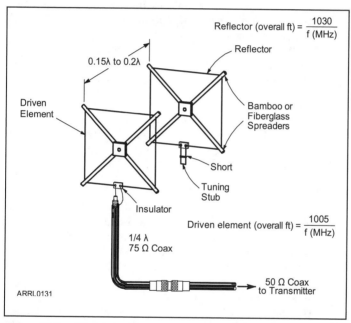

**Figure G9.8 — The construction of a quad antenna. The lengths of the driven element and reflector element are given by the equations shown in the drawing. To find the length of one side, divide these total lengths by four.**

**G9C14   How does the forward gain of a two-element quad antenna compare to the forward gain of a three-element Yagi antenna?**

A. About the same
B. About ⅔ as much
C. About 1.5 times as much
D. About twice as much

**(A)**    A two-element quad (or delta loop) antenna has about the same gain as a three-element Yagi. [*General Class License Manual*, page 7-15]

**G9C15   What is meant by the terms dBi and dBd when referring to antenna gain?**

A. dBi refers to an isotropic antenna, dBd refers to a dipole antenna
B. dBi refers to an ionospheric reflecting antenna, dBd refers to a dissipative antenna
C. dBi refers to an inverted-vee antenna, dBd refers to a downward reflecting antenna
D. dBi refers to an isometric antenna, dBd refers to a discone antenna

**(A)**    Antenna gain figures are all relative to some reference antenna. Gain in dBi is gain relative to an isotropic antenna that radiates equally in all directions. Gain in dBd is gain relative to the maximum gain of a ½ wavelength dipole antenna in free space. [*General Class License Manual*, page 7-3]

**G9C16   What is a beta or hairpin match?**

A. It is a shorted transmission line stub placed at the feed point of a Yagi antenna to provide impedance matching
B. It is a ¼ wavelength section of 75 ohm coax in series with the feed point of a Yagi to provide impedance matching
C. It is a series capacitor selected to cancel the inductive reactance of a folded dipole antenna
D. It is a section of 300 ohm twinlead used to match a folded dipole antenna

**(A)**    The beta match (or "hairpin") shown in **Figure G9.7C** is a short length or "stub" of parallel conductor transmission line connected directly across the driven element feed point. The stub acts as an inductive reactance that can compensate for any capacitive reactance at the feed point. [*General Class License Manual*, page 7-12]

# G9D — Specialized antennas

**G9D01**   Which of the following antenna types will be most effective as a Near Vertical Incidence Sky Wave (NVIS) antenna for short-skip communications on 40 meters during the day?

A.  A horizontal dipole placed between ¹⁄₁₀ and ¼ wavelength above the ground

B.  A vertical antenna placed between ¼ and ½ wavelength above the ground

C.  A left-hand circularly polarized antenna

D.  A right-hand circularly polarized antenna

**(A)**      NVIS, or Near Vertical Incidence Skywave, refers to a communications system that uses low, horizontally polarized antennas such as dipoles that radiate most of their signal at high vertical angles. These signals are then reflected back to Earth in a region centered on the antenna. NVIS allows stations to communicate within the skip zone that exists for lower-angle sky wave propagation. [*General Class License Manual*, page 7-7]

**G9D02**   What is the feed point impedance of an end-fed half-wave antenna?

A.  Very low

B.  Approximately 50 ohms

C.  Approximately 300 ohms

D.  Very high

**(D)**      Feed point impedance of a ½-wavelength dipole increases as the feed point is moved away from the center and is several thousand ohms at the ends. The end-fed half-wave (EFHW) antenna with its feed point at one end is popular for portable operating because it is lightweight and easy to install. [*General Class License Manual*, page 7-3]

**G9D03**   In which direction is the maximum radiation from a portable VHF/UHF "halo" antenna?

A.  Broadside to the plane of the halo

B.  Opposite the feed point

C.  Omnidirectional in the plane of the halo

D.  Toward the halo's supporting mast

**(C)**      The halo antenna is a dipole bent into a circle or square (the "squalo") with the ends separated by a small gap. The halo radiates most strongly in the plane of the antenna. Halos are usually mounted horizontally so they produce an omnidirectional pattern with the horizontal polarization preferred for VHF weak-signal operation. [*General Class License Manual*, page 7-15]

**G9D04    What is the primary purpose of antenna traps?**

A.  To permit multiband operation
B.  To notch spurious frequencies
C.  To provide balanced feed-point impedance
D.  To prevent out-of-band operation

**(A)**    Traps are parallel LC circuits that act as electrical switches at their resonant frequencies to isolate sections of the antenna. At other frequencies, traps act as inductance or capacitance. This changes the antenna's "electrical length" automatically, allowing it to operate on two or more bands. [*General Class License Manual*, page 7-19]


**G9D05    What is an advantage of vertical stacking of horizontally polarized Yagi antennas?**

A.  It allows quick selection of vertical or horizontal polarization
B.  It allows simultaneous vertical and horizontal polarization
C.  It narrows the main lobe in azimuth
D.  It narrows the main lobe in elevation

**(D)**    The increase in gain for a vertical stack of Yagi antennas results from narrowing the vertical width of the main lobe of a single antenna's radiation pattern. The narrower lobe results in stronger received signals and less received noise at angles away from the peak of the main lobe. [*General Class License Manual*, page 7-17]


**G9D06    Which of the following is an advantage of a log periodic antenna?**

A.  Wide bandwidth
B.  Higher gain per element than a Yagi antenna
C.  Harmonic suppression
D.  Polarization diversity

**(A)**    A log-periodic antenna is designed to provide consistent gain and feed point impedance over a wide frequency range. [*General Class License Manual*, page 7-17]


**G9D07    Which of the following describes a log periodic antenna?**

A.  Element length and spacing vary logarithmically along the boom
B.  Impedance varies periodically as a function of frequency
C.  Gain varies logarithmically as a function of frequency
D.  SWR varies periodically as a function of boom length

**(A)**    The name "log periodic" refers to the ratio of length and spacing between adjacent elements of the antenna. By designing the antenna entirely in terms of ratios, the antenna's performance becomes independent of frequency over a wide range. [*General Class License Manual*, page 7-17]

**G9D08** How does a "screwdriver" mobile antenna adjust its feed-point impedance?

A. By varying its body capacitance
B. By varying the base loading inductance
C. By extending and retracting the whip
D. By deploying a capacitance hat

**(B)** The "screwdriver" antenna design — a whip with an adjustable loading coil at the base — has gained popularity for HF mobile operation as a good compromise between performance and convenience. The name derives from the small dc motors typical of electric screwdrivers used to adjust the loading coil. [*General Class License Manual*, page 7-6]

**G9D09** What is the primary use of a Beverage antenna?

A. Directional receiving for low HF bands
B. Directional transmitting for low HF bands
C. Portable direction finding at higher HF frequencies
D. Portable direction finding at lower HF frequencies

**(A)** Beverage antennas are most effective at frequencies of 7 MHz and below. This includes the amateur MF (medium frequency) 160 meter band, as well as the lower HF bands of 80, 60, and 40 meters. [*General Class License Manual*, page 7-17]

**G9D10** In which direction or directions does an electrically small loop (less than ⅓ wavelength in circumference) have nulls in its radiation pattern?

A. In the plane of the loop
B. Broadside to the loop
C. Broadside and in the plane of the loop
D. Electrically small loops are omnidirectional

**(B)** If the circumference of a loop is less than ⅓ wavelength, current in the loop becomes relatively uniform all the way around the loop. This results in a radiation pattern with sharp nulls broadside to the plane of the loop. [*General Class License Manual*, page 7-15]

### G9D11 Which of the following is a disadvantage of multiband antennas?

A. They present low impedance on all design frequencies
B. They must be used with an antenna tuner
C. They must be fed with open wire line
D. They have poor harmonic rejection

**(D)** Multiband antennas by definition are designed to radiate well on several frequencies. Most HF amateur bands are harmonically-related, meaning their frequencies are integer multiples of each other — 3.5, 7, 14, 21, and 28 MHz. While this is convenient in that one antenna can be used on separate bands, harmonics of a fundamental signal on, for example 7 MHz, will be radiated well by a multiband antenna on 14, 21, and 28 MHz. [*General Class License Manual*, page 7-19]

### G9D12 What is the common name of a dipole with a single central support?

A. Inverted V
B. Inverted L
C. Sloper
D. Lazy H

**(A)** A dipole needn't be straight to be effective. Using a single antenna support, a dipole supported in the center makes it easy to attach the feed line. This configuration is called an "inverted V." [*General Class License Manual*, page 7-4]

### G9D13 What is the combined vertical and horizontal polarization pattern of a multi-wavelength, horizontal loop antenna?

A. A figure-eight, similar to a dipole
B. Four major loops with deep nulls
C. Virtually omnidirectional with a lower peak vertical radiation angle than a dipole
D. Radiation maximum is straight up

**(C)** When the circumference of a loop reaches multiple wavelengths, there can be many current peaks and nulls along the loop. These create many lobes and nulls in the radiation pattern. The result is an essentially omnidirectional pattern with the peak angle of radiation somewhat lower than a dipole at the same height. [*General Class License Manual*, page 7-13]

# Electrical and RF Safety

Your General class exam (Element 3) will consist of 35 questions taken from the General class question pool as prepared by the Volunteer Examiner Coordinators' Question Pool Committee. A certain number of questions are taken from each of the 10 subelements. There will be 2 questions from the subelement shown in this chapter. These questions are divided into 2 groups, labeled G0A and G0B.

## SUBELEMENT G0 — ELECTRICAL AND RF SAFETY
## [2 Exam Questions — 2 Groups]

### G0A — RF safety principles, rules and guidelines; routine station evaluation

**G0A01    What is one way that RF energy can affect human body tissue?**
A.  It heats body tissue
B.  It causes radiation poisoning
C.  It causes the blood count to reach a dangerously low level
D.  It cools body tissue

**(A)**    Body tissues subjected to very high levels of RF energy may suffer heat damage. These effects depend on the frequency of the energy, the power density of the RF field that strikes the body, and even on factors such as the polarization of the wave. The thermal effects of RF energy should not be a major concern for most radio amateurs because of the relatively low RF power we normally use and the intermittent nature of most amateur transmissions. It is rare for amateurs to be subjected to RF fields strong enough to produce thermal effects unless they are fairly close to an energized antenna or unshielded power amplifier. [*General Class License Manual*, page 9-9]

**G0A02** Which of the following properties is important in estimating whether an RF signal exceeds the maximum permissible exposure (MPE)?

A. Its duty cycle
B. Its frequency
C. Its power density
D. All these choices are correct

**(D)** The body's natural resonant frequencies affect how the body absorbs RF energy. For this reason, polarization, power density and the frequency of the radio signal are all important in estimating the effects of RF energy on body tissue. [*General Class License Manual*, page 9-9]

**G0A03** How can you determine that your station complies with FCC RF exposure regulations?

A. By calculation based on FCC OET Bulletin 65
B. By calculation based on computer modeling
C. By measurement of field strength using calibrated equipment
D. All these choices are correct

**(D)** You may use any of these three procedures to determine whether your station complies with the exposure guidelines. The simplest, by far, is to perform the calculations in FCC OET Bulletin 65. There are online and software tools to help you perform the calculations. In complex or unique situations, it may be required to model or measure the exposure. [97.13(c)(1)] [*General Class License Manual*, page 9-12]

**G0A04** What does "time averaging" mean in reference to RF radiation exposure?

A. The average amount of power developed by the transmitter over a specific 24-hour period
B. The average time it takes RF radiation to have any long-term effect on the body
C. The total time of the exposure
D. The total RF exposure averaged over a certain time

**(D)** Time averaging, when applied to RF radiation exposure, takes into account the total RF exposure by averaging it over either a 6-minute or a 30-minute exposure time. Time averaging compensates for the transmit/receive time ratio during normal amateur communications. It takes into account that the body cools itself after a time of reduced or no RF radiation exposure. [*General Class License Manual*, page 9-10]

**G0A05** **What must you do if an evaluation of your station shows RF energy radiated from your station exceeds permissible limits?**

A. Take action to prevent human exposure to the excessive RF fields
B. File an Environmental Impact Statement (EIS-97) with the FCC
C. Secure written permission from your neighbors to operate above the controlled MPE limits
D. All these choices are correct

**(A)** Some of the things you can do to prevent human exposure to excessive RF radiation are to move your antennas farther away, restrict access to the areas where exposure would exceed the limits, or reduce power to reduce the field strengths in those areas. [*General Class License Manual*, page 9-13]

**G0A06** **What precaution should be taken when installing a ground-mounted antenna?**

A. It should not be installed higher than you can reach
B. It should not be installed in a wet area
C. It should be limited to 10 feet in height
D. It should be installed such that it is protected against unauthorized access

**(D)** The best precaution for installing antennas is that people should not be able to come in contact with them. No one should be near a transmitting antenna while it is in use. Install ground-mounted transmitting antennas well away from living areas so that people cannot come close enough to be exposed to more than the MPE limits. If there is a possibility of someone walking up to your antenna while you are transmitting, it may be a good idea to install a protective fence around the antenna. [*General Class License Manual*, page 9-13]

**G0A07** **What effect does transmitter duty cycle have when evaluating RF exposure?**

A. A lower transmitter duty cycle permits greater short-term exposure levels
B. A higher transmitter duty cycle permits greater short-term exposure levels
C. Low duty cycle transmitters are exempt from RF exposure evaluation requirements
D. High duty cycle transmitters are exempt from RF exposure requirements

**(A)** Since amateurs usually spend more time listening than transmitting, low duty cycles are common. Remember that including duty cycle in the exposure evaluation takes into account the reduced average transmitted power from not operating continuously at full power. This means greater short-term exposure levels can be permitted with low-duty-cycle emissions. [*General Class License Manual*, page 9-11]

**G0A08** Which of the following steps must an amateur operator take to ensure compliance with RF safety regulations when transmitter power exceeds levels specified in FCC Part 97.13?

A. Post a copy of FCC Part 97.13 in the station
B. Post a copy of OET Bulletin 65 in the station
C. Perform a routine RF exposure evaluation
D. Contact the FCC for a visit to conduct a station evaluation

**(C)** Even if your station is exempt from the requirement, you may want to do a simple RF Radiation Exposure Evaluation. The results would demonstrate to yourself and possibly to your neighbors that your station is within the guidelines and is no cause for concern. None of the actions listed in the other answer choices would help to ensure that your station meets the FCC RF safety regulations. [*General Class License Manual*, page 9-12]

**G0A09** What type of instrument can be used to accurately measure an RF field?

A. A receiver with an S meter
B. A calibrated field strength meter with a calibrated antenna
C. An SWR meter with a peak-reading function
D. An oscilloscope with a high-stability crystal marker generator

**(B)** You can use a calibrated field-strength meter and calibrated field-strength sensor (antenna) to accurately measure an RF field. Even if you have access to such an expensive laboratory-grade field-strength meter, several factors can upset the readings. Reflections from the ground and nearby conductors (power lines, other antennas, house wiring, etc.) can easily confuse field-strength readings. You must know the frequency response of the test equipment and probes, and use them only within the appropriate range. Even the orientation of the test probe with respect to the polarization of the antenna being tested is important. [*General Class License Manual*, page 9-12]

**G0A10** What is one thing that can be done if evaluation shows that a neighbor might receive more than the allowable limit of RF exposure from the main lobe of a directional antenna?

A. Change to a non-polarized antenna with higher gain
B. Post a warning sign that is clearly visible to the neighbor
C. Use an antenna with a higher front-to-back ratio
D. Take precautions to ensure that the antenna cannot be pointed in their direction

**(D)** A simple way to ensure that you do not point your antenna toward a neighbor's house while you are transmitting is to clearly mark your rotator control to remind you. Some rotator controls also have programmable "no go" regions that can prevent rotating the antenna to those directions. [*General Class License Manual*, page 9-13]

**G0A11** **What precaution should you take if you install an indoor transmitting antenna?**

A. Locate the antenna close to your operating position to minimize feed-line radiation
B. Position the antenna along the edge of a wall to reduce parasitic radiation
C. Make sure that MPE limits are not exceeded in occupied areas
D. Make sure the antenna is properly shielded

**(C)** You should locate any antenna (whether it is indoors or outdoors) as far away as practical from living spaces that will be occupied while you are operating. You should also perform a routine environmental evaluation to make sure that MPE limits are not exceeded in occupied areas. [*General Class License Manual*, page 9-14]

## G0B — Station safety: electrical shock, safety grounding, fusing, interlocks, wiring, antenna and tower safety

**G0B01** **Which wire or wires in a four-conductor connection should be attached to fuses or circuit breakers in a device operated from a 240 VAC single phase source?**

A. Only the two wires carrying voltage
B. Only the neutral wire
C. Only the ground wire
D. All wires

**(A)** The hot wires (the wires carrying voltage) are the only ones that should be fused. If fuses are installed in the neutral or ground lines, an overload will open the fuses or circuit breaker but will *not* remove power from any equipment connected to that circuit. [*General Class License Manual*, page 9-5]

**G0B02** **According the National Electrical Code, what is the minimum wire size that may be used safely for wiring with a 20 ampere circuit breaker?**

A. AWG number 20
B. AWG number 16
C. AWG number 12
D. AWG number 8

**(C)** AWG number 12 wire is required for a 20-ampere circuit. [*General Class License Manual*, page 9-5]

**G0B03** Which size of fuse or circuit breaker would be appropriate to use with a circuit that uses AWG number 14 wiring?

A. 100 amperes
B. 60 amperes
C. 30 amperes
D. 15 amperes

**(D)** AWG number 14 wiring should be protected by a 15-ampere fuse or circuit breaker. [*General Class License Manual*, page 9-5]

**G0B04** Which of the following is a primary reason for not placing a gasoline-fueled generator inside an occupied area?

A. Danger of carbon monoxide poisoning
B. Danger of engine over torque
C. Lack of oxygen for adequate combustion
D. Lack of nitrogen for adequate combustion

**(A)** Carbon monoxide and other exhaust fumes can accumulate in your garage, basement or other confined living area, so ventilation is very important. Be sure not to place generators near air intakes or vents, as well. [*General Class License Manual*, page 9-7]

**G0B05** Which of the following conditions will cause a Ground Fault Circuit Interrupter (GFCI) to disconnect the 120 or 240 Volt AC line power to a device?

A. Current flowing from one or more of the voltage-carrying wires to the neutral wire
B. Current flowing from one or more of the voltage-carrying wires directly to ground
C. Overvoltage on the voltage-carrying wires
D. All these choices are correct

**(B)** A GFCI opens the circuit if it detects an imbalance in the currents flowing through the hot and neutral leads. The imbalance indicates that some current is bypassing the neutral connection. That is a serious shock hazard and should be located and repaired. [*General Class License Manual*, page 9-6]

**G0B06** **Which of the following is covered by the National Electrical Code?**

A. Acceptable bandwidth limits
B. Acceptable modulation limits
C. Electrical safety inside the ham shack
D. RF exposure limits of the human body

**(C)** The National Electrical Code covers the wiring of electrical devices, [*General Class License Manual*, page 9-4]

**G0B07** **Which of these choices should be observed when climbing a tower using a safety belt or harness?**

A. Never lean back and rely on the belt alone to support your weight
B. Confirm that the belt is rated for the weight of the climber and that it is within its allowable service life
C. Ensure that all heavy tools are securely fastened to the belt D-ring
D. All these choices are correct

**(B)** As you are climbing up or down, remember to take your time — it's not a race! Be sure your climbing gear is fully secure:

• Belts and harnesses must be within their service life and adequately rated for weight

• Carabiners should be completely closed

• Latching hooks should close away from the tower

• Always use a safety lanyard or redundant lanyards

And remember that often forgotten rule to follow the manufacturer's directions! [*General Class License Manual*, page 9-15]

**G0B08** **What should be done by any person preparing to climb a tower that supports electrically powered devices?**

A. Notify the electric company that a person will be working on the tower
B. Make sure all circuits that supply power to the tower are locked out and tagged
C. Unground the base of the tower
D. All these choices are correct

**(B)** Before climbing, remove power from any circuit that will not be used while you are on the tower. The best way is to remove fuses or open circuit breakers. Once the circuit is opened, lock the circuit breaker open, if possible, and tag the fuse block or breaker panel so that no one will reconnect the circuit. [*General Class License Manual*, page 9-15]

**G0B09**   **Which of the following is true of an emergency generator installation?**

A.  The generator should be located in a well-ventilated area
B.  The generator must be insulated from ground
C.  Fuel should be stored near the generator for rapid refueling in case of an emergency
D.  All these choices are correct

**(A)**      See G0B04. [*General Class License Manual*, page 9-7]


**G0B10**   **Which of the following is a danger from lead-tin solder?**

A.  Lead can contaminate food if hands are not washed carefully after handling the solder
B.  High voltages can cause lead-tin solder to disintegrate suddenly
C.  Tin in the solder can "cold flow," causing shorts in the circuit
D.  RF energy can convert the lead into a poisonous gas

**(A)**      Lead is a known toxin when ingested or inhaled. Although the amount of soldering done by most amateurs does not cause enough lead exposure to be a hazard, it is a good idea to wash your hands after soldering and not eat "at the bench." [*General Class License Manual*, page 9-3]


**G0B11**   **Which of the following is good practice for lightning protection grounds?**

A.  They must be bonded to all buried water and gas lines
B.  Bends in ground wires must be made as close as possible to a right angle
C.  Lightning grounds must be connected to all ungrounded wiring
D.  They must be bonded together with all other grounds

**(D)**      Lightning protection grounds must be tied to all other safety grounds in your home and shack. Having separate ground systems can expose equipment to damage from the lightning current jumping between ground systems. [*General Class License Manual*, page 9-8]

**G0B12    What is the purpose of a power supply interlock?**

    A. To prevent unauthorized changes to the circuit that would void the manufacturer's warranty

    B. To shut down the unit if it becomes too hot

    C. To ensure that dangerous voltages are removed if the cabinet is opened

    D. To shut off the power supply if too much voltage is produced

**(C)**    High voltages are often present inside transmitter and amplifier power supplies. The interlocks on those supplies prevent you from coming in contact with energized power supply components. Interlocks often short high voltage circuits to ground when activated, providing further safety measures. Do not defeat or bypass interlock circuits unless the repair instructions specifically require you to do so. [*General Class License Manual*, page 9-6]

**G0B13    What must you do when powering your house from an emergency generator?**

    A. Disconnect the incoming utility power feed

    B. Insure that the generator is not grounded

    C. Insure that all lightning grounds are disconnected

    D. All these choices are correct

**(A)**    If you do not disconnect your home's circuit breaker box from the incoming power line, called backfeeding, the power from your generator will flow back to the utility lines where it creates a shock hazard for utility workers. In addition, if utility power is restored with your generator connected to the power line, the generator may be damaged. [*General Class License Manual*, page 9-7]

**G0B14    What precaution should you take whenever you adjust or repair an antenna?**

    A. Ensure that you and the antenna structure are grounded

    B. Turn off the transmitter and disconnect the feed line

    C. Wear a radiation badge

    D. All these choices are correct

**(B)**    One way to be sure that no one can activate the transmitter while you are working on it is to turn off the transmitter power supply and disconnect the antenna feed line. If there is a chance of anyone entering the station, it is also a good idea to post a notice that you are working on the antenna. [*General Class License Manual*, page 9-15]

MOSLEY ANTENNAS

**Mosley**

AIRCRAFT GRADE ALUMINUM ELEMENTS & BOOMS and STAINLESS STEEL HARDWARE

...*"a better Antenna!"*

**STRONG!**
Snow, ice or rain are no match for Mosley Quality!

...*built to last!*

Call **800-325-4016**

**REQUEST A CATALOG**
www.mosley-electronics.com
or
www.mosleyelectronics.com

**ARRL Members Get it All!**

**Online Benefits**

- *QST* Digital Edition
- FREE E-Newsletters
- *QST* Archive and Periodicals Index
- Product Review Archive
- E-Mail Forwarding Service

**ARRL** The national association for AMATEUR RADIO®
www.arrl.org/join

*HamTestOnline*™ *students are 50 times more likely to give us 5 stars than request a refund because they failed an exam!*

**eHam.net reviews**
★★★★★ 758
5.0 out of 5 stars

| | |
|---|---|
| 5 star | 737 |
| 4 star | 18 |
| 3 star | 2 |
| 2 star | 1 |
| 1 star | 0 |

*The best study method, customer support, and guarantee in the industry!*
**www.hamtestonline.com**

# Ready to Upgrade?

When you complete the final step up the Amateur Radio license ladder, you'll enjoy full privileges on all frequencies that come with earning your Amateur Extra Class license. Our expert instruction will lead you through all the knowledge you need to pass the exam. **Achieve the highest level today!**

The ARRL
**Extra Class License Manual**
For Ham Radio

**All You Need to Pass Your Extra Class Exam!**

**NEW! Eleventh Edition**

- Pass the 50-question Extra Class exam
- All the exam Questions with Answer Key, for use through June 30, 2020.
- NEW! Use with ARRL's Online Exam Review for Ham Radio.
- Detailed explanations for all questions, including FCC Rules.

| LEVEL 1 Technician | LEVEL 2 General | LEVEL 3 Amateur Extra ✓ |

**Convenient Spiral Bound Edition!**

| LEVEL 1 Technician | LEVEL 2 General | LEVEL 3 Amateur Extra ✓ |

# ARRL Will Help!

The ARRL Extra Class License Manual
Spiral Bound — Eleventh Edition
ARRL Item No. 0550. **Only $32.95**

- All the exam questions with answer key, for use through June 30, 2020.
- Spiral Bound Edition lies flat.
- Use with ARRL's **Online Exam Review for Ham Radio.**
- Detailed explanations for all questions, including FCC Rules.

The digital edition is available in the Kindle format from Amazon.

**Order Online at www.arrl.org/shop**
or call Toll-Free
**1-888-277-5289**

**ARRL** The national association for AMATEUR RADIO®
225 Main St. Newington, CT 06111-1400

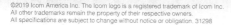